ROOF OF THE WORLD

ROOF OF THE WORLD
Man's First Flight Over Everest

James Douglas-Hamilton

MAINSTREAM
PUBLISHING

This edition published by
MAINSTREAM PUBLISHING COMPANY (EDINBURGH) LTD.
25 South West Thistle Street Lane
Edinburgh EH2 1EW

ISBN 0 906391 38 5

The publisher acknowledges the financial assistance of the Scottish Arts Council
in the publication of this volume.

Cover and book design by Jenny Carter
Front cover illustration by John Hewitt
Printed and bound in Great Britain by
Spectrum Printing Company, Edinburgh

CONTENTS

ACKNOWLEDGEMENTS

The author and publishers wish to thank the following, who have kindly given permission for the use of copyright material:— Constable and Company Limited, for extract from *Lucy Houston DBE: One of the Few* by Warner Allen; Brian and David Blacker for extracts from *Pathans, Planes and Petards* by Stewart Blacker; Jarrolds for extracts from *The Last Strongholds* by Colonel P.T. Etherton; and *The Times* for permission to quote extracts. The publishers have been unable to trace the copyright holders of some extracts and regret that acknowledgement for these cannot be made in this edition.

The author also wishes to thank David and Brian Blacker; Mrs Mayura Brown, the Vice-President of the Britain-Nepal Society; Wing Commander Noel Capper AFC; Herbert de Grey; Lord Hugh and Lord Patrick Douglas-Hamilton; Richard Ellison; Mrs. Carlyle Gifford; the Duke of Hamilton; Elizabeth, Duchess of Hamilton; John Hewitt; Baron Hunt KT, CBE, DSO; John Longley; David McConnell; Don Mclean; Dugal McIntyre; John Mutch of Biggart Baillie & Gifford; Harald Penrose; Air Commodore Henry Probert MBE of the Air Historical Branch of the Ministry of Defence; Alan Robertson; T.D.M. Robertson; Earl of Selkirk KT, GCMG, GBE, AFC, AE; Lord Tweedsmuir CBE, LLD; R.A. Watt; the staff of the Ministry of Defence Adastral Library; and the staff of the House of Commons Library for their assistance.

The Publishers gratefull acknowledge the following for permission to use the photographs in this book:—
The Duke of Hamilton, pages 23, 31, 32, 33, 38, 56, 59, 67,69,71,76, 77, 78 top & bottom, 82, 83, 85, 86, 88 top & bottom, 89, 91, 94, 95, 97, 99, 103, 106, 107 top & bottom, 124, 126,127 top & bottom, 134, 138, 153
The Times, pages 36, 45, 47, 48, 50 top & bottom, 64, 71, 102
Rt. Hon. Lord Tweedsmuir, page 16
Keystone Press Agency, pages 49, 51
Mrs Carlyle Gifford, 170
Mrs Mayura Brown, 68
Richard Ellison, pages 73, 101, 109, 131, 137, 151, 167
Lord Hunt, page 142
Royal Geographical Society, page 145
Brian and David Blacker, pages 18, 19, 25, 48, 63, 72, 75, 84, 93, 111, 120
Paul Popper Ltd, pages 8, 14, 40, 46, 98
R. Watt, pages 168, 171
George Outram, page 153

MOUNT EVEREST

High on the roof of the world, long lapped in dreaming
where the eternal snows are cold and deep—
Cold and deep and a glacier black and gleaming—
Cradled in cloud, Everest lies asleep.
. . . . .
Now from below in the first fair flush of the dawning,
On stronger wings than ever an eagle bore,
Up through the blue immensity of the morning
Two man-made eagles soar.
. . . . .
And the frozen air is cleft by man's contriving,
And the silver silence is shattered by man's machine,
And men exultant see the end of striving—
The virgin peak where never a man has been.

M. Pardoe in *The Saturday Review*.
8 April 1933.

Everest, half hidden by the shoulder of Chamlang, Makalu on the right

FOREWORD

The Rt. Hon. Lord Tweedsmuir C.B.E., LL.D.

THIS BOOK IS by the son of the chief pilot of the highly successful and hazardous Houston Mount Everest Expedition of 1933. It tells of how four men, in two single-engined bi-planes were the first in history to look down on and photograph the top of Mount Everest. The writer is my son-in-law.

In June 1932 his father, then the Marquis of Douglas and Clydesdale M.P. was approached by my own father, John Buchan, who was then M.P. for the Scottish Universities, and asked if he would lead such a venture if it proved possible to launch it. My father had been a very fine climber in his youth, and was a member of the Alpine Club. He wrote a book called *The Last Secrets,* containing a chapter on Mount Everest which was then unclimbed. He never lost his interest in exploration and I have seen him in the Rocky Mountains in Canada when he was well into his sixties, planning in his mind's eye the routes he would have taken on those towering peaks. But of all mountains Mount Everest fascinated him most. Its upper slopes were at that time still unseen by mortal eye.

Clydesdale appealed to him because he had youth and vitality and was a distinguished and skilful airman commanding 602 (City of Glasgow)

Bomber Squadron in the Auxiliary Air Force. He was also a superbly fit young man. He had been stroke of the Balliol VIII, captained the Oxford Boxing team, was a good skier and had been middleweight boxing champion of Scotland. Almost every moment of his spare time was spent flying with the Auxiliary Air Force. He had a burning conviction that the air was his element. He seemed to my father to be an altogether natural choice as Chief Pilot, and a man for such a challenge.

If any should wonder why men are drawn to such hazardous adventures, the answer lies in the words of that great polar explorer, Fridtjof Nansen: "A mighty manifestation of the power of the unknown over the mind of men".

Until 1856 Everest was one of a series of almost unapproachable Himalayan peaks and was dignified, not by a name but, merely a number: Peak XV in fact. It was christened after a Surveyor General of India called Sir George Everest, and from its christening it has held mystery and magnetism for the rest of the world. It had by 1933 drawn a number of climbing expeditions, claimed not a few lives, and was still unconquered. This mountain with a very English name seemed a personal challenge to the people of this country. The magnetic pull of the mountain has never diminished.

Flying then was still in its infancy. People were just getting used to the world having a new dimension, once described as an "uninterrupted navigable ocean that comes to the threshold of everyman's door". At that time Britain had achieved the records for flying the greatest distance, at the maximum speed and to the highest altitude yet attained. But already Admiral Byrd had ridden this new element to the North and South Poles, and Britain was feeling the challenge. A committee was formed. Clydesdale and my father were members and 14 months of intensive work went into the planning to keep four human beings in the air over Everest for 15 minutes. In the course of this study aviation took considerable strides.

On April 4th, 1933, the two single-engine planes took off from Purnea on the 150-mile flight to the peak of Everest. Looking back there were so many things without which the expedition could never have been begun. One was finance. All through this century expeditions have been funded by private subscription, generally coming from many pockets and involving the knocking on many different doors. Those of us who knew Clydesdale remember his charming diffidence and very real shyness. He would have found this distasteful and difficult. It was therefore the greater gain that the financial generosity of Lady Houston, whom he approached, put all financial worries behind them. The other equally fundamental necessity was gaining permission of the Nepal government to fly over their territory.

But there were so many other factors that had brought them to this jumping-off point. The most powerful ingredient of success was the excellence of the team under their wise and experienced leader, Air Commodore Fellowes and the individual calibre of the pilots and observers which made it a practical proposition. Fellowes had insisted that the minimum should be left to chance, and that they must do all their thinking on the ground, and work out as far as possible every conceivable situation with which they could be faced in the air. Their flight from Britain to North Africa and then across India to their starting point was an epic in itself. It took them across an older India, an Omar Khayam tapestry of Maharajahs and palaces and peacocks, tigers and temples.

From the moment that morning when they took off to climb through the many thousands of feet of the dust haze of the Indian plains to reach the clear mountain air this becomes a story of four people. Clydesdale and his observer/photographer Colonel Blacker were in one plane. Blacker's grandfather had been the first Surveyor General of India. He had ended a distinguished career by killing an adversary in a duel, and falling dead from his adversary's bullet, at the same instant. To his grandson, this expedition was a long held ambition. Clydesdale would pilot the leading aircraft with Blacker as Chief Observer and the other aeroplane would be flown by Flight Lieutenant David McIntyre, a brother officer in the same Squadron, with an extremely experienced aerial photographer called Bonnett.

This was no ordinary adventure for adventure's sake, neither was it just a desire to get in first, although that came into it. Many experts had worked on these planes and the splendid Pegasus engines were far ahead of their time. But the fact remains that they would only photograph Everest, and return, if they had unusually favourable weather conditions. The Pegasus engines could carry the aircraft at 140 miles per hour at that height, but the winds are often far stronger than that. They reckoned it would take them 1½ hours to reach Everest and they would have enough petrol then to stay for 15 minutes and no more. They took no parachutes, but reckoned that they could possibly glide for 75 miles if the engine failed. The cockpits were open, and to keep alive at that altitude, which would almost instantly extinguish human life, they had to wear electrically warmed clothing and oxygen apparatus. Daunting conditions.

The photographers had to perform 46 different tasks if they were to bring back the results which they hoped.

Only a few hours later they returned. But it must have seemed like days to those who were awaiting them on the ground. What the flyers had seen struck them with a force of revelation. Accounts written by men whose normal speech was the simple English of everyday life reached high flights of lyrical description. Clydesdale wrote of the sighting of Everest from above the heat haze 50 miles away, "the dust haze, completely obscuring the foothills, rose well above the snow line with the result that this arc of great mountains appeared detached from the earth and suggested an eerie land floating in a drab sea somewhere between earth and sky". None of them were ever to forget that scene, or how close they came to disaster when a down-draught caught them and sent them hurtling downwards to clear a long knife-edge ridge far too closely to bear thinking about. In a very few hours they were back at their base again.

It would probably be quite wrong to assume that people read forewords. For those that may, I will not spoil the end of the adventure, and the act of "magnificent insubordination" which justified its undertaking. The expedition takes its place among the great pioneering sagas of the history of aviation.

1 THE GREAT CHALLENGE

THE SMOKING ROOM of the House of Commons was almost deserted on that summer evening in June 1932, but for two figures huddled together beside the window overlooking the Thames. Anyone who had caught a glimpse of them might have imagined they were discussing Britain's political problems, from the Gold Standard and Employment prospects to proposals for constitutional development in India.

However their thoughts were far removed from such matters. With much deliberation the older of the two men was putting a proposal to his younger companion, who was listening intently and saying very little. Their conversation, in fact, concerned the unlikely topic of the highest mountain in the world, Mount Everest, and the contrast between the comfort of the Smoking Room and the desolate scene of biting winds tearing around its summit seemed immense.

Their fascination for the grim mountain which had already claimed the lives of thirteen men was very great. It stood as a symbol of all that was most inaccessible and they knew its story intimately. . . .

In the heart of the Himalayas, the most mighty range of mountains in the world, 1600 miles long, 150 miles broad in the East and 300 miles in the West, lay this mountain, surrounded by rock bastions, freezing glaciers and towering cliffs. For centuries it had been virtually unknown to mankind, until one day in 1856 Radhanath Sikdar, a Bengali Chief Computer, rushed into the office of Sir Andrew Waugh, the new Surveyor-General of India. His statement was brief but momentous: "Sir I have discovered the highest mountain in the world".[1] He pointed to the mountain-top named Peak XV on the map.

Sir Andrew Waugh checked the figures and confirmed the fact. Peak XV, at a height of over 29,000 feet, was indeed the highest point in the world. But to call such a mountain by a number appeared ridiculous, and Sir Andrew turned his attention to giving it a name. He might have named it after the first Surveyor-General of India, Colonel Valentine Blacker. Instead, after some thought, he chose to call it Mount Everest after his immediate predecessor.

From that time Everest, as the Queen of Himalayas, represented one of the last strongholds of nature, unseen by the eye of man. It caught the attention of the public, and when Sir Francis Younghusband and the Royal

Rongbuk Monastery and Mount Everest

Geographical Society recommended that it should be climbed, Younghusband declared that "Everest stands for all that is highest and finest and most difficult of attainment."[2]

As it was extremely hard to approach from the South across the vast glaciers in Nepal, a reconnaissance expedition was sent to gain access to Everest from the Rongbuk Valley to the North of the mountain, in Tibet. There the monks at the Rongbuk Monastery had no name for what was believed to be a sacred mountain. "Birds cannot fly so high"[3] was their only reference to it.

This 1921 Expedition included George Mallory, a brilliant climber with an iron physique and great powers of endurance. He helped to trace what appeared to be the best route to the summit and named the Col on the North Ridge, the North Col. By the end of the year they had mapped out the country to the North of Everest.

In 1922 a climbing expedition under General Bruce tried to carry out the ascent of the mountain, Mallory again being one of the climbers. Three assaults on the mountain were attempted. On the first Mallory, with two other climbers, reached the height of 26,985 feet without oxygen. On the second occasion oxygen was used and the climbers mounted to a height of 27,300 feet. The third time disaster struck, when an avalanche swept seventeen of the climbers down the mountain. Mallory was one of the survivors to witness the loss of several of his friends.

In 1924 greater heights than ever were reached in an epic endeavour with which the names of Mallory and Irvine, the renowned Oxford athlete, will always be remembered. On 8 June Odell watched Mallory and Irvine going straight for the summit. From 26,000 feet he could see the two men moving rapidly on the ridge, leading to Everest's crest, within a few hundred feet of the top. Then the mist came down and a snow cloud surrounded them, and from that day to this, no man ever saw Mallory or Irvine again.

Odell went off in search of them the next day with winds howling around him and reached 27,000 feet, in itself a notable climb. But nowhere was there anything to be seen. Nor were Mallory and Irvine the only victims. In the same expedition a young Gurkha died from exposure and a Tibetan from pneumonia and frostbite. In all, by 1933, Mount Everest had claimed the lives of thirteen men who had hoped to scale its heights.

When Mallory had been asked why he wished to climb Mount Everest, he had replied, "Because it is there".[4] He had known the dangers, and had sought to pit man's spirit against the forces of nature. His example would be followed: already plans were being made by Hugh Ruttledge to lead another Expedition to climb Mount Everest in 1933.

By that time Everest had already been assaulted from both land and air. Sir Alan Cobham, the well-known British aviator who had flown for the first time from London to Cape Town and back, had tried to fly over the mountain in 1924, but without oxygen he came nowhere near to succeeding. Later on he had flown from England to Australia and back, landing on his return on the Thames on 26 October 1926 in front of the Houses of Parliament, not far from where the two men were speaking in the House of Commons. . . .

Cobham's flight had been one of the events to trigger off the interest of the older M.P., himself a man with an adventurous disposition, who had

John Buchan M.P.

written more than 50 books and who represented the Scottish Universities. His name was John Buchan, author of *The Thirty Nine Steps* and a host of other popular yarns. Born the son of a Scots Minister he had always set his sights on broad horizons. Words flowed from him. The man he was speaking to was the second youngest M.P. in Parliament, the Marquis of Clydesdale, a former Scottish Amateur Middleweight Boxing Champion, who in his spare time from the House of Commons had flown extensively, becoming the youngest Squadron Leader in the Auxiliary Air Force, commanding the 602 (City of Glasgow) Bomber Squadron.

Buchan knew of Clydesdale as a man of excellent physical fitness, who was held in high regard as a pilot. Now he was telling him that Cobham had not been the only aviator to try to surmount Everest in the air. Early in 1932 Richard Haliburton and Meyro Stevens, two American airmen had made the attempt, but they had succeeded in flying no higher than 15,500 feet, just over half Everest's height. There were also indications that German and French aviators were going to try as soon as they possessed suitably developed aircraft.

This led to John Buchan's proposal. It was essential in his view that British aircraft and pilots should fly over Mount Everest first, establishing a leading role in world aviation. Since the Britons, Alcock and Brown, had flown the Atlantic in 1919, Americans and others had tended to be in the forefront of world aviation. It had been an American, Admiral Byrd, who had flown over both the North and the South Poles, and Britain in recent years had not played as big a pioneering role in geographical exploration as she might have done. He hoped that Clydesdale would consider becoming the Chief Pilot of an Expedition to make the first flight by man over Mount Everest.

In Buchan's thinking, the proposed Expedition would obtain invaluable air survey photographs of scientific and geographical interest. From these it would be possible to map the unknown Southern side of Everest, and to establish that there was no part of the world over which aircraft could not fly. Consequently in the future the world's most inaccessible mountains could be traced and mapped. In any case the Expedition would be of considerable assistance to the British Aviation Industry, by proving that Britain was able to produce the world's most advanced aircraft with oxygen apparatus and photographic equipment, which had never been used for operational flights at such heights before.

It would, of course, be extremely dangerous. The slightest miscalculation or technical failure with the oxygen or engine or fuel would almost certainly be fatal, and no-one knew how treacherous the mighty blasts of hurricane winds might be around the summit, or of the rising and falling currents of air. Even so, with all the pitfalls and disadvantages, this project lay just within Britain's technical capability, and John Buchan hoped that Clydesdale would agree to serve.

Clydesdale had listened with care to the unfolding of this saga. Although an active and energetic constituency M.P. he knew that in some ways the

Colonel Stewart Blacker O.B.E. with oxygen apparatus and heated goggles

political circumstances he found himself in favoured his participation in the Everest scheme. In 1931 the National Government had come to power with a massive majority, and as one of its supporters he had begun to feel that "one individual counted for little among so many, and that he might be as usefully engaged in examining the India question on the spot".[5] The prospect of seeing India and of answering such a challenge was irresible. Bleriot had been the first pilot to fly the Channel and Lindbergh had been the first to fly the Atlantic solo, but no aircraft had come near to flying over Mount Everest. From what John Buchan had told him there might be the possibility of proving the worth of British machinery and equipment, and of making a contribution to scientific development. He agreed to serve.

Almost immediately he received an invitation to join the 1932 British

Colonel Stewart Blacker O.B.E. whose idea the flight was

Flight to Mount Everest Committee. There he met Colonel Stewart Blacker, Lord Peel who was Blacker's father-in-law, and Colonel Etherton. He realised at once that Colonel Blacker, who always wore a monocle, was a forceful dynamic and courageous man. His enthusiasm for this flying expedition, which was originally his idea, amounted to a lifelong ambition. His grandfather, Colonel Valentine Blacker, the first Surveyor-General of India had been responsible for mapping Hindustan, using the triangulation method of theodolites. Being a somewhat volatile individual Colonel Valentine Blacker had taken part in a duel in which both he and his opponent were killed. He was succeeded some years later as Surveyor-General by one of his disciples, Sir George Everest. The work started by Valentine Blacker continued and much of India and a small part of the Himalayas were mapped.

Colonel Stewart Blacker himself had had a remarkable career. An Officer in the Indian Army before the First World War, he learned to fly in 1911. After the outbreak of war he took part in the fighting in the trenches and was hit by German machine gun fire. On recovering he transferred to the Royal Flying Corps in 1915. He was shot down twice while flying low over enemy lines, and with an inventor's zeal he tested an aircraft to see if a machine gun could fire over the propellor. Unfortunately the experiment on this occasion did not succeed. The aircraft crashed and he sustained a fracture of the cervical vertebrae.

After convalescence he rejoined the Army, and became the only officer to command an independent force in the Great War as a Captain. In 1919-1920 he served as an acting Lieutenant Colonel with the Corps of Guides in Khorasan. There he was attacked by a Kurdish-Soviet force, and after a swift engagement the enemy, or rather those of them who survived, were routed. For this campaign his soldiers were awarded a medal with two clasps by a special Army Order. Blacker himself was mentioned in Despatches and on 8th May 1922 he received the Military Order of the British Empire for valuable services rendered in connection with minor military operations in North and North East Persia. He had extensive knowledge of India and Central Asia, and on retiring from the Regular army early in 1932, he had been given the command of a Field Artillery Battery in the Territorial Army.

One of his comrades in the trenches had been Colonel Etherton, who had travelled widely in the Himalayas and China. He was a charming, efficient and highly articulate organiser, with a feel for diplomacy. In 1910 he had made his way from India to Russia, through Chinese Turkestan, Mongolia and on to Siberia. He used a route which had not been used before, making his way with the assistance of carts, camels, horses, yaks and sledges. As an explorer he knew much about the whole range of the Himalayas, separating the two most numerous races in the world, and after the war he had served as British Consul-General in Chinese Turkestan. His Indian Army Unit had been the Royal Garhwal Rifles, and after fighting in the trenches his Army service took him to Egypt and Mesopotamia, where he received a Mention in Despatches and then on to Russian Turkestan.

As for Lord Peel, he had worked out that the Expedition would somehow have to assemble near Purnea, under the Himalayas, for the momentous flight, and had assessed the kind of ground which would have to be flown over if the necessary permission were forthcoming.

Purnea was in Bihar, where the fields were cultivated and indigo was grown. But on the way to the North towards Everest the peaceful atmosphere of the Indian plains would give way to a virtually impenetrable jungle in which the tiger and the rhinoceros roamed. Flying across this zone, called the Terai, seared as it was with deep gorges and foothills, would take only a few minutes, and then the aircraft would be over Nepal, the land of the Gurkhas. In this territory the mountains would be covered in vegetation, with tea plantations at their lower levels. The mountainsides would be thick with pine trees, rhododendrons and birch. Beyond them the greenery would be overtaken by areas of turf streaked with boulders and the beds of torrents long dried-up. Above them would be rocks and cliffs of Himalayan peaks disappearing into the depths of the sky, overshadowed by the mighty glaciers of Chamlang. Surpassing them were immense mountains and enormous areas of snow, rock and ice; and towering over them all, in its grim and terrible splendour, was the South face of Everest where no man had ever set his foot and which no man had seen as a whole. It was over this awesome scene that Clydesdale would have to fly, if they could get the Expedition off the ground.

It was essential that there should be two aircraft with observers in order to bring back the necessary scientific results. Already a certain amount of preparation had been completed. The Headquarters of the Committee had been located at the College of Aeronautical Engineering in Chelsea. In March 1932, Blacker had submitted proposals to the Royal Geographical Society, listing his aims as follows:—

I. To reconnoitre and to map by air photographic survey the almost unknown Southern slopes of the massif of Mount Everest, thereby making an important contribution to Geography, and to its allied sciences.

II. To produce a cinematograph film of exceptional attraction and real worth, not only to science, to the world and education in general, and to combine with this the creation of a new height record for an aeroplane carrying two persons, thereby adding value to both achievements.

III. To carry out these feats with purely British personnel and thereby to give a stimulus to enterprise.[6]

In April 1932, the Royal Geographical Society gave its blessing to the proposed Expedition and wrote to the Secretary of State for India that they thought that the plan would probably lead to valuable scientific results. The next step forward was to obtain the support of the Air Ministry, where the plans, diagrams and charts for the Expedition were sent. The Air Council decided to give unofficial backing, and offered to the Expedition's organisers the facilities of the Royal Air Force School of Photography at the Royal Aircraft Establishment at Farnborough, and at the Royal Air Force Experimental Establishment at Martlesham. Furthermore negotiations were set in hand with the Bristol Aeroplane Company, in the hope that Pegasus engines could be used.

In May an official application to fly over Nepal was made by the India Office, impressing on the Maharajah of Nepal that valuable results might be obtained for scientific and geographical purposes. The fact that the India Office, the Air Ministry and the Royal Geographical Society supported the Expedition was noted by the Government of Nepal, which did not send an immediate reply.

Colonel Etherton, being an old friend of the British Envoy in Nepal, learnt that their proposal was receiving serious and sympathetic consideration by the Nepalese Government in the capital, Kathmandu. He had arranged at the same time for the landing ground at Lalbalu near Purnea to be used by the Expedition, and an Air Survey Plan for mapping the area to the South of Everest was drafted with the Geographical Section of the War Office's General Staff.

As soon as Clydesdale joined the Committee it was decided that the IS3 Pegasus engine which had established a new world altitude record should be used for the flights. Blacker was convinced that with its supercharger it was ideal for the purpose, as it had the power to carry a pilot and an observer with oxygen, camera and electrical heating installations.

Everything progressed smoothly through the summer months. The India Office was approached to ask for the loan of a reserve pilot and various other skilled RAF personnel in India as well as for exemption from customs duties for the necessities of the Expedition. During this period approaches were made to ensure physical and financial support for the operation.

Clydesdale approached the Shell Oil Company. John Longley was working in Shell's International Aviation office, and found himself interviewing Clydesdale, who had arrived without any appointment. Longley recalled:

> I was personally greatly flattered to find myself talking freely to a senior RAF officer—a mendicant marquis at that—and I a pilot officer on the reserve . . . I was not sure whether the interviewer or interviewee was the more conscious of the importance of the occasion and the more uncertain of the correct procedure.
>
> His [Clydesdale's] purpose was to persuade Shell to sponsor the Everest flight that he was undertaking, although he never got round to disclosing the measure of support he envisaged . . . He dilated enthusiastically on the venture, was ineffably polite and not very incisive about his begging mission. . . . However free fuel was duly granted for the . . . flight, in return for free publicity, despite Shell's policy of not supporting financially RAF flights.[7]

Clydesdale was anxious that the fuel should be able to perform at extreme altitude. The problem was solved by the chemists of Shell collaborating with the makers of the Bristol Aeroplane Company, to produce a blended fuel, which could function in all circumstance. As for oil, Wakefield's Castrol Aero Coil proved to be adequate, and steps were taken to ensure that necessary fuel supplies would be laid along the route to the base camp in India.

It was a boost for the morale of the Committee to learn that the Peninsular and Oriental Steam Navigation Company would transport two large aircraft free of charge to Karachi and back, and would give concessionary rates to members of the Expedition travelling by sea. Imperial

Airways also offered favourable rates to those connected with the Expedition. This generosity was accompanied by support from Messrs Fry, the chocolate manufacturers who decided to lend one of their light aircraft, to act as a reconnaissance aeroplane. With this aircraft came chocolates, which could come in useful in returning hospitality, as well as being a welcome addition to their diet of Sanatogen food, which would be taken from Britain.

Their Lawyers would be Messrs Baddeleys; their travel agents Messrs

The Marquis of Douglas and Clydesdale M.P., youngest squadron leader in the Auxiliary Air Force.

Thomas Cook and Son and their accounts would be handled by Messrs Deloitte Plender Griffiths and Company. With their help it became an interesting feature of the Expedition that everything in the form of equipment was of British manufacture. Messrs Thomas Black and Sons from Greenock had provided camp equipment, tents and kit, designed for rough travelling and strenuous circumstances. The Monitor Oil Appliances supplied the camp stove which would operate in wind and extreme cold.

Even the more personal items came without exception from British sources. Their clothing, of the toughest and most durable kind suitable for a hot climate came from Gieves. Watches which would function under all known conditions likely to be encountered were obtained from Rolex. Cameras which could guarantee to take good photographs in tropical conditions were considered essential, and six-twenty Kodaks were selected. Finally in case they were attacked by crocodiles or other forms of game Rigby Mannlicher rifles able to shoot with extreme accuracy, would be included with the other items to be taken out to India.[8]

At the same time as the Secretary of the Expedition, Colonel Etherton was persuading firms to be generous, the Gaumont British Picture Corporation entered into negotiations with the Committee on the basis that they would like to film the Expedition and its work.

In August the news arrived that the Nepalese Government had given permission under certain conditions. There were to be no practice flights over Nepal, full notice had to be given of the great flight, and there was to be no aerial survey of Nepal, other than that associated with Mount Everest and its surrounding mountains and glaciers.

The Maharajah wished to be informed before the flight and immediately afterwards of the results. This news was received with delight, since Colonel Etherton had been under the impression that there was concern in Kathmandu, in case one or both of the aircraft were to crash in the lower reaches of Nepal.

By mid-September much of the technical planning had received approval but the obtaining of funds was still a considerable hurdle. The total cost of the expedition would be in the region of £19,000, and the contribution of companies and individuals had not been more than a few thousand pounds. The financial crisis in 1932 had curtailed much of the anticipated financial assistance. For various reasons the minds of the organisers turned to Lady Houston, one of the world's richest women who had put up £100,000 so that Britain and British pilots could compete with other nations for the Schneider Trophy Contest, which British pilots proceeded to win. Furthermore Lady Houston was an aquaintance of Clydesdale's mother. Clydesdale was detailed to go and see her at her home at Byron Cottage, Hampstead.

Some months before the Committee had approached Lady Houston but a meeting had not been arranged, owing to her illness. She responded to the second overture, agreeing to see Clydesdale, as she thought that such a flight, were it to succeed, would greatly redound to the credit of the British

Lady Houston D.B.E., whose generosity made the expedition possible

aviation industry. Her chief concern was doubt as to whether the Expedition could succeed, and when Clydesdale arrived she decided to listen without committing herself. Clydesdale wrote: "She listened to my brief statement and then turned away from it, without giving me any assurance, to resume her discussion of political matters which were clearly her main interest. She did not, however, attempt to pour cold water on the idea and decline to give it her support. I was immensely impressed with the intensity of her patriotism and the fervour of her feeling for Great

Britain and the Empire. I felt that there was no sacrifice however great she would not be prepared to make in order to strengthen British prestige throughout the world or to set the British Empire more firmly on its foundations."[9]

Lady Houston sometimes appeared to act on impulse but in reality she held her own counsel until she had obtained the best expert advice, before making a final decision. It was on account of her uncertainty that she had switched the conversation on to subjects concerned with the Empire and politics. Whilst Clydesdale awaited a response from her as to whether the project could go ahead, suddenly, on 24 September, to his dismay, the story broke in the Scottish Press that the M.P. for East Renfrewshire had been selected as Chief Pilot of the British Expedition to fly over Mount Everest, and that it would set out as soon as possible after September. It was also revealed that the two aircraft would have special engines and special breathing apparatus to enable them to rise to the height of 35,000 feet.

The *Paisley and Renfrew Gazette,* widely read in his Constituency, had traced him to the home of Lord Londonderry, the Secretary of State for Air. He admitted his interest in the flight, but would not confirm that he would make the attempt, saying "There is many a slip twixt the cup and the lip."[10] He stated that if he did make the attempt, his aim would be to further the interests of aviation in Britain, believing as he did that British aircraft and engines numbered among the best in the world. He said that he was anxious to see aircraft manufacture being extended in England, and he looked forward to the creation of a Scottish Aviation Industry.

When this unwelcome publicity appeared, not only had his Constituency Chairman, Provost Michie, not been informed that he wished to ask for permission for three months' leave, but the finances of the Expedition were not in order. He had intended to contact his Constituency Chairman once the financial arrangements had been put on a sound footing, and he still was not in a position to confirm that the Expedition would go ahead.

He received a letter from Michie to the effect that everyone in East Renfrewshire who had spoken to him was wholeheartedly opposed to their M.P. "taking part in the affair".[11] Several influential people had stated that if there was any truth in the matter a meeting of the Constituency Executive would have to be called to appoint a Deputation, to persuade Clydesdale to withdraw from the Expedition altogether.

It seemed as if Clydesdale's hopes to meet the great challenge placed before him by John Buchan that day in the House of Commons' Smoking Room were to be dashed, even before the Expedition had really begun.

2 A TIDE OF SUPPORT

THE PUBLICITY IN the Scottish national press accelerated the speed of development and a meeting of the East Refrewshire Conservative Association was arranged for 5th October in Paisley Town Hall, so that Clydesdale might appear before his constituents to request permission for three months' leave of absence to take part in the Mount Everest Air Expedition. Even in 1932 such a request from an M.P. to his Constituency Association was virtually unheard of, and there were indications of strong opposition.

Then, just when matters seemed to be most bleak and forbidding, he received a message from that powerful woman, Lady Houston. She wished to see him. The recent publicity had roused her interest and she invited him to stay at her home, Kinrara in the Scottish Cairngorms. When he arrived there she was ill and confined to bed, but she gave him a conclusive promise of financial support.

He soon learned that her motives in wanting the Expedition to succeed were not the same as his own. As he wrote about the earlier meeting, "She gave me no inkling of the idea which may already have begun to germinate in her mind, that the flight intended as a serious contribution to the Science of Aviation and as a Survey of remote regions, might be made to serve a political end by impressing a native population in India with the courage, endurance and vigour of the new generation of Britons. I had no thought of playing the heroic impersonator of British youth."[1]

As Lady Houston saw it, here might be an opportunity to raise the prestige of Britain in India, and therefore every effort must be made to have an extremely efficient organisation. Clydesdale must in particular take advice from Wing Commander Orlebar, who had trained the two British pilots who won the Schneider Trophy, and who was a complete expert in this field.

On his return home Clydesdale was struck down with influenza, and therefore, being unable to address the meeting in Paisley Town Hall, he drafted a letter to his Constituency Chairman, Provost Michie, setting out the case for the Expedition. Now he was in a stronger position, with Lady Houston having made herself responsible for the finances, and he had reason to hope that the Duke of York would give his patronage. In addition, both the India Office and the Air Ministry were giving support.

On 5th October, 1932, his Secretary appeared before a packed audience in Paisley Town Hall to read out the letter, with representatives from every Branch in the East Renfrewshire Constituency attending. Major Michie D.S.O., Provost of Renfrew and Chairman of the Conservative Association presided, and the audience listened with fascination to see how their M.P. could justify his extraordinary request. The letter ran:

A short time ago I offered my services as pilot to the Expedition. The Committee considered my name along with others, and I was selected as Chief Pilot, subject to the Air Ministry's sanction and approval of my satisfactorily carrying out all the practical altitude tests.

The Medical Board of the Air Ministry have categorised me as "an exceptionally suitable type" physically.

Some members of this Constituency have shown concern as regards the danger of this project. I have full considered this side also, and would like to assure you that I have no wish to subject this Constituency again to the expense and trouble of a by-election.

About 50 miles of this flight is over impossible country, on which one must rely on one's engine. The objects of the Expedition are, first and foremost, to foster and promote British prestige in the world, and especially in India.

Americans have flown over the North Pole and the South Pole, the Pacific Ocean has been crossed by air, and the Atlantic has been frequently flown.

There is only one original flight really worth while; that is the flight over Mount Everest, which alone stands out as the only significant part of the world which has not been flown over.

The success of the flight will have a great psychological effect in India. It will do much to dispel the fallacy that this country is undergoing a phase of degeneration, but rather instil the truth that Britain is ready to pass through a process of regeneration. It will show India that we are still a virile and active race, and can overcome difficulties with energy and vigour, both for ourselves and for India.

This great enterprise seemed doomed to failure until Lady Houston, always ready to further and promote the prestige of Britain, saved the situation.

We all remember well Lady Houston's magnificent and generous gesture when she enabled Britain to win outright the Schneider Trophy, and retain our reputation for having accomplished the greatest speed in the world. I feel that the people of this country do not yet realise what we owe to Lady Houston.

Lady Houston is making herself entirely responsible for the finance of this scheme. She is doing so not in any way as a stunt, but for her patriotic love of Britain and what Britain stands for.

My taking part in a venture of this kind will mean strenuous training and absence from this country for some time. It will mean that I shall not be able to give my attention to the Constituency's affairs as much as I would otherwise have done; but I would say that a very large number of M.P.s are businessmen and have their business to attend to as well as their Constituency. I have no commercial business, and I think I can honestly say that I devote more time to this Constituency than do most M.P.s to theirs.

I feel that this is an opportunity in which I can really be of some service to my country. It is something big, and well worth doing, and doing properly, even at the expense of having to be away for some time from East Refrewshire and the House of Commons.[2]

It had been a long letter, and it was followed by a spontaneous series of speeches from the representatives of each part of the Constituency. Far from condemning him, according to *The Scotsman* newspaper, all the speeches commended their M.P. on his courage. By unanimous decision the meeting resolved to give him leave of absence, wishing him God-speed and a safe return.

The letter had been written, putting the case strongly, stressing that this was the last really significant flight to be made over the highest point on the world's surface. It was quoted in full in the press, and aroused a complaint from a Congress member of the Assembly in India, in opposition to the probable psychological consequences of the flight. But for all that the hurdles of receiving financial support and of obtaining permission from the Constituency were cleared.

Lady Houston's offer was to fund the Expedition up to the extent of the very large sum of £10,000, with a guarantee of another £5,000. On the day he received this undertaking Clydesdale met Blacker and Etherton at the College of Aeronautical Engineering. Thinking themselves to be in dire financial straits, they had been discussing the prospect of hiring an aircraft from a company, under circumstances which would effectively have placed the venture in the control of that company.

On his arrival Clydesdale listened with displeasure to the company's representatives outlining their proposals. They would provide the pilot and the aircraft, leaving the equipment and photographer to the two Colonels to organise. Clydesdale maintained his silence till they left, and then broke the news to Blacker and Etherton about their new financial strength. "The whole situation changed. From the jubilation which succeeded the pessimism of a few minutes before, it might have been concluded that all practical difficulties were surmounted. We now had no excuse for improvisation or making shift."[3] Nor did they have too much time to celebrate: there was so much still to do.

The best expert assistance was obviously required for the many details which had to be checked, cross-checked and tested. Blacker and Clydesdale were in touch with the Secretary of State for Air, Lord Londonderry, who introduced them to the Chief of the Air Staff, Air Chief Marshal Sir John Salmond. At once Salmond saw the need to appoint an experienced senior officer who would help to coordinate the detailed technical and scientific planning of the Expedition. Without hesitation he recommended Air Commodore Fellowes as an ideal leader and a dedicated airman who had much experience in flying in countless countries and climates, including mountainous territories.

Fellowes had been highly decorated in the First World War and had won a bar to the Distinguished Service Order he received because of the part he played in a sortie to drop a large bomb on the lock gates at Zeebrugge. The task had been considered so dangerous and important that Fellowes undertook to do it himself in preference to any junior officer. Not long afterwards he was wounded and captured.[4] After the war, he became involved in airship development, acting as Director from 1924 to 1929 when the airships R100 and R101 were constructed. He had even helped to establish aerodromes in Persia during his career, and after retiring from active service still flew in his spare time whenever he could. Here was a man able to demand the very highest standards from those in the British Aeronautical Industry with whom the Expedition would be involved.

On 11th November the Air Commodore was appointed leader of the Expedition. He was easy to work with and knew how to get the best out of those working under him, welding them into a team. He was meticulous in preparation, taking over the executive organisation. He believed in leaving nothing to chance and ensured that hundreds of tasks were carried through. Colonel Etherton assisted him ably as the Secretary for the Expedition and helped to reduce the costs, and to conserve what resources they had. Taking responsibility for the whole enterprise came naturally to Fellowes, and acting on Clydesdale's recommendation that Flight Lieutenant David McIntyre was an outstanding Flight Commander in the 602 (City of Glasgow) Bomber Squadron, he selected McIntyre as the second pilot.

Gradually the planning for the Expedition was coming together, the maxim of Air Commodore Fellowes being that all thinking must be done on the ground, and that it was infinitely preferable to check out every possible eventuality relating to the oxygen and aircraft, even if it caused delay, rather than take any precipitate action in the air. His calm, steady

Flight Lieutenant David McIntyre, flight commander of 602 (City of Glasgow) Bomber Squadron

assurance and consistent resolution gave confidence to everyone.

The Expedition at this time was receiving a great deal of publicity—and it was favourable. One article which appeared on 21st October, in the

Tangier Gazette in Morocco, and later in the *Evening Telegram* in Newfoundland and in the *Civil and Military Gazette* in India, summed up in a few words what much of the British press was saying:

Flying men have never planned a more picturesque endeavour than the assault on Mount Everest. The world's height record, established by Mr. Cyril Uwins in a British biplane is 43,976 feet, nearly three miles higher than the summit. But the mountain lies remote in the heart of a terrific range of peaks many of which rival it in stature, in a region where a forced landing would mean destruction and where blow winds of hurricane force.

Further, the head of the giant is the home of tremendous storms and vast frozen cloud masses shroud the peak from view for many months of the year. The men who take off . . . are beginning one of the most perilous adventures in the history of Aviation . . .

Like all truly great adventurers, Lord Clydesdale and his comrades have made careful plans, and while recognising the perils before them, believe in their own ability, linked with the trustworthiness of their flying equipment, to overcome them.

A period of intensive training and flying trials must precede embarkation for India. Each member of the party must attain the perfection of physical fitness to withstand the ardours of flying above the Himalayas.

The interior of the fuselage showing the heated oxygen cylinders

Aeroplanes and engines must be perfectly attuned to the task, there will be no room for a single mechanical failure. Indeed only the astonishing dependability attained in recent years by the British aero engine put the enterprise within the limits of reasonable endeavour.[5]

With such sentiments in mind Air Commodore Fellowes had made arrangements for the pilots and observers to go to the Royal Aircraft Establishment at Farnborough to test their oxygen equipment, before the aircraft had been assembled for the test flights. The Eagle and cine cameras would also have to checked, so that they had experienced, at experimental centres, conditions even more extreme than those which would exist in the vicinity of the Everest summit.

Fellowes, Blacker, Etherton and Clydesdale were marshalling their plans with a torch-bearing zeal, and were receiving a great deal of support. They believed in what they were doing passionately. They foresaw that the process of travel and distribution would in the future not be restricted to the land and sea, but would be extended to the air, and they knew that their country had a large part to play. Later they would write:

Air is the universal element. The spirit of the world is changing and its problems are new. Speed is the key-note of life—speed and energy. A new calling has come into being, which is really the spirit of the old pioneers aflame in a new form . . . transport by air, the uninterrupted navigable ocean that comes to the threshold of every man's door.[6]

The cockpit of the Houston Westland

3 CONFRONTING THE DANGERS

THERE WERE A great many dangers which the pilots would have to reckon with. If there was a hitch in relation to any one of a hundred parts of their chosen aircraft, disaster could follow. The winds of hurricane force in the vicinity of Everest and the possibility of oxygen failure were further threats ever present in their minds.

Colonel Blacker had asked the Chief of the Air Staff, Sir John Salmond, to confirm his approval for the use of the Bristol Pegasus IS3 engine, similar to the one with which flight Lieutenant Uwins won the world altitude record of 43,976 feet. This time the purpose was different. The world altitude record had been obtained by one pilot in a single-seater aircraft. On the Houston Mount Everest Flying Expedition an observer would be needed as well, with a considerable number of cameras and other equipment for an operational flight. The aircraft would have to gain the necessary height, with the required film and oxygen supplies, at a time when the wind levels were sufficiently low to make the flight possible.

Sir John Salmond gave his approval for the use of the Pegasus engine, which would give the aircraft a flying speed of 140mph at 35,000 feet. But even with the strength of this engine, if the winds above Everest were running at 140 mph, it would be impossible for the aircraft in its most advanced stage of development to make any headway against it. The Expedition could, therefore, only succeed if all the circumstances, including the wind speeds, were favourable. The Pegasus engine represented a safe start. It was an air-cooled radial engine with nine cylinders, supercharged so that it could function at full power at very high altitude. It operated inside a Townend ring cowling, whose effect was to introduce a measure of streamlining, for the purpose of reducing wind resistance. This addition might add an extra 10 mph. It was believed that the Pegasus was the only engine in the world capable of taking an aircraft over Mount Everest.

The Bristol Aeroplane Company was asked to produce first one engine and then another, as it was thought that the Expedition would complete its aims more efficiently with two aircraft than with one. The company agreed to allow their mechanic, Cyril Pitt, to go with the Expedition, to look after the Pegasus engines. The next step was to choose the aircraft which would be suitable for the engines. They decided to go to the Westland Aircraft Company at Yeovil.

Their interest in the Westland Aircraft Company had been kindled by Flight Lieutenant Uwins, who had won the world altitude record, and who was the Test Pilot at the R.A.F. Experimental Establishment at Martlesham. Uwins had recommended that Clydesdale should look at the Westland PV3, as it had the fastest climb of any two-seater aircraft which the R.A.F had ever tested. The Westland PV3 and the Westland Wallace came up to their expectations.

The Westland PV3 was an experimental military aircraft, capable of photo-reconnaissance and bombing, or of carrying a torpedo. It was unique, since as soon as it was built, the specification for it was altered. The Westland Wallace was similar in many respects to the PV3, and had been adopted as a general purpose machine for the Royal Air Force to replace the Westland Wapiti, the prototype from which both of these aircraft was developed. No less than nineteen Squadrons in the R.A.F. had been equipped with the Wapiti, and it had been used a great deal for flying in India, particularly over the high mountains near the North West frontier.

The Committee were aware that as well as the two Westland aircraft the Vickers Vespa was the only other aircraft capable of such a mission. It was thought that it would be better to have two aircraft made by the same company, to make servicing easier. They decided to order the PV3, to be specially named the Houston Westland, and the Wallace, which the pilots would later nickname "Lucy" and "Akbar".

Just as they had made their decision, in November 1932, the Irish Defence Ministry kindly offered two Vickers Vespa aircraft, which they had to decline. The aircraft they had selected were altogether suitable. They had a high undercarriage, were able to take the Pegasus engine, had a wide wing span of 46½ feet with a large wing area giving climbing capacity,

Left, the Houston Westland and right, the Westland Wallace, being adapted at Yeovil to fly over Mount Everest

and the fuselage was wide and deep; the two aircraft were each 34 feet in length. Here were machines capable of carrying whatever would be required; and the Westland Aircraft Company agreed to send Francis Burnard, an experienced mechanic, with the Expedition.

The aircraft would have to be adapted. The bomb racks and gun ring would have to be removed, saving some weight. With skilful flying, brakes would be unnecessary. The two aircraft would each be able to carry 1400 lbs on setting out, fuel weighing 700lbs on take off. By the time they arrived at the summit of Everest they would each have used up 380 lbs of fuel, and would have less than fifteen minutes around the summit if they were to return without running out of fuel.

Everest was 160 miles from Purnea where they would have their base camp, and if there was engine failure the aircraft might glide up to 70 miles so they would be within gliding distance of level country for two-thirds of their track. They decided to take no parachutes, to save weight, which meant that if they were to survive there could be no scope for any kind of engine failure near Everest. In this connection the Bristol Aircraft Company and the Burmah Shell Company Limited took great trouble to provide specially concocted fuel, which would not freeze at great heights.

This would be available at Lalbalu airstrip near Purnea, as well as at the different aerodromes between Karachi and Purnea, since the aircraft would be shipped to Karachi as soon as construction and test flights were completed.

In order to keep the engine cool, Castrol experts drew up a "temperature chart", which would give the mechanics in India the chance to adjust the cooling to suit the conditions of that climate. The pilots would have preferred to have had more than one engine in the event of failure, but it was not practicable at that stage of aircraft development. The airscrew would be driven at half the speed of the crankshaft which would improve efficiency on take-off. There would be one propeller made of wood, of large diameter, so that it would take a strong grip of the air at high altitude. With this propeller, the speed of the aircraft at low levels over the ground would be 77 mph, rising to 135 mph in level flights at operational height, the speed for landing being just over 50 mph. It was expected that climbing time would be six minutes to 10,000 feet, 13 minutes to 20,000 feet and 25 minutes to 30,000 feet.

Being biplanes, spring control boxes had to be fitted because the wings and most of the frame were constructed from duralumin and the control cables were made of steel. At great heights the duralumin was known to contract twice as much as the steel, so spring control boxes were fitted on to the control cable, to enable the pilot to have maximum control.

Care was taken in the design of the aircraft to protect the pilot and observer from icy winds. In front of the pilot's open cockpit was placed a large windscreen of triplex glass. In front of both the pilot and the observer was a three-ply partition. The observer's cockpit could be entirely enclosed, with two roof panels in position. If the observer wished to stand up to take a photograph, he could fold these panels inwards, fixing them to one side. There was a window on each side of the observer, and the floor had sliding panels, so that a camera could point downwards through the bottom of the observer's cockpit on the terrain below. The side windows could be opened outwards on hinges as well, again in such a way as to protect the observer from the slip-stream.

The Williamson Automatic Eagle III Survey cameras would take photographs at regular intervals through the flight, to obtain from overlapping photographs a mosaic of the strip flown over. The flights to Everest and back should be over mountains, including a number of known points fixed by ground survey. From the photographs it was hoped that an accurate and detailed map of contour lines of a considerable area could be drawn. The Eagle Survey Camera contained fine lenses and 450 working parts, operating from a small electric motor driven by the 1000-watt generator in the aircraft. The film wound from one spool to another after timed exposures. The timing of exposures would be controlled by a knob to be operated by the pilot or observer, the interval between the 125 exposures in the magazine being as little as six seconds or as much as a minute. If each picture overlapped the next picture by two-thirds of its length, it was necessary to take more photographs at low level to obtain the necessary overlap. This meant that at a height of 10,000 feet each picture had to be taken every twenty seconds, and when the aircraft was actually near Everest's summit, photographs would be taken every six seconds, the intervals being diminished in stages as the ground came closer.

A spirit level was installed in the camera, so that the observer could ensure that the camera was level to the ground. Made almost entirely of duralumin and in order to combat the extreme cold the cameras had to be covered with an electrically heated jacket, electric wires being connected with plugs and leads sewn into it. There were four such jackets, one for the body of the camera, one for the lens which was fitted once the camera was in its mounting rig, one for the magazine in the camera and one for the spare magazine.

The observer in the first aircraft—the Houston Westland—namely Colonel Blacker, the Chief Observer, would take one survey camera, two still cameras for oblique rather than vertical photographs and one Sinclair Newman cine camera. The observer with the second aircraft would take one survey camera, one still camera and two Sinclair-Newman cine cameras.

Agreement had been reached with the Gaumont-British Film Corporation, allowing them to send two cameramen, who had been selected after exhaustive physical and technical examination. The cameraman chosen to fly with McIntyre for the first attempt on Mount Everest was Bonnett, who had flown with Sir Alan Cobham on many of his long distance flights in Africa. The other photographer was Fisher, who had previously descended in a submarine to photograph the ocean bed.

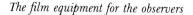

The film equipment for the observers

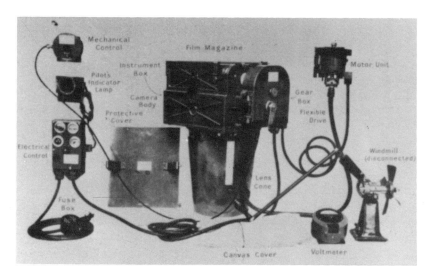

Together they were sent by Air Commodore Fellowes on 26th January 1933 to the Dartford Works of Messrs J. and E. Hall Limited, the refrigerating engineers. There they put on electrically heated flying suits, heated boots and heated gloves. They were invited to enter a refrigerating chamber with one Williamson Eagle Camera and with two cine cameras, each of the cameras being covered with a heating jacket.

Bonnett walked first into an airlock and then into the freezing chamber beyond. He stayed there for thirty minutes at minus 40 degrees centigrade, operating the cameras. The electricity heating his clothing and the jackets for the cameras reduced the cold to minus 30 degrees centigrade, and the temperature had to be made colder for Fisher who followed him. They knew that extreme cold would have made the film brittle and liable to break, with jamming of cameras and clouding of lenses, but the heating was so effective that these problems had not occurred. The tests had been satisfactory, and not only would they be taking photographs of areas never seen before, but they would also have 8000 feet of new high-speed infra-red film, to enable clearer pictures to be taken.

Earlier in the month the pilots had been subjected to medical tests and experiments in a sealed chamber to check their oxygen apparatus. It was imperative that they were extremely fit physically, and the medical examination was designed to discover whether they could stand up to severe and prolonged physical and mental stress. The pilots would have to be able to respond effectively in any crisis in the interest of both their own lives and those of their observers.

The R.A.F. Central Medical Board had a number of ingenious tests. Each pilot had to blow into a tube, to force a column of mercury to rise in a glass, and to hold it at that level for as long as possible. They were told to breathe deeply and exhale into a spirometer, and were then ordered to hold their breath as long as they could. They were seated in chairs which revolved ten times in twenty seconds, to see if they would lurch sideways, the purpose being to find out how they would perform in a spin by the aircraft towards the ground. A metal rod, similar to a pencil, was placed on a board pointing upwards. This had to be lifted with the rod remaining in position. Another test was for each of them to stand for fifteen seconds on one leg with eyes shut. They had three chances to pass these tests, and Clydesdale and McIntyre passed them easily.[1]

The Medical Tests had been stringent, since in the event of any difficulty with oxygen, extreme fitness might fend off unconsciousness for some time. It was, of course, the case that climbers had ascended to over 28,000 feet on Mount Everest without oxygen, but as they climbed over a prolonged period of several weeks they became acclimatised and the lungs of the climbers became accustomed to a higher altitude. It would be quite different for a pilot who could climb in an aircraft from the ground to above 30,000 feet in about half an hour. If a pilot attempted to do this without oxygen, his body could not stand up to the strain. He would have some warning before lapsing into unconsciousness, by experiencing

Ready for high altitude, looking like a figure from outer space

sensations not dissimilar to those of being anaesthetized. On becoming unconscious the aircraft would go out of control. Above the Himalayas an uncontrolled aircraft would in all probability collide with a mountain or glacier long before the aircraft reached a sufficiently low level for the pilot to recover consciousness.

Sir Robert Gorman of Messrs Siebe Gorman had invented the oxygen equipment for the aircraft. Three 750-litre cylinders had been prepared to carry oxygen, and these were to be installed in racks in the fuselage of each aeroplane. The cylinders were made from vibrac, a steel of great strength, and a series of copper and aluminium pipes were connected to it.[2] The oxygen had to pass from the cylinders down the piping to a gauge which revealed the pressure in the cylinder, and from there on to the regulator, which contained a valve enabling the pilot to increase or reduce the pressure. It then reached the electrical heating equipment, consisting of a coil of electric wire surrounding the piping. The oxygen would move on to the flow-meter, which would show the rate of flow along the pipe. All the pilot was required to do was to adjust the value of the regulator, so that the reading of the altimeter of the aeroplane corresponded to the required reading of the flow-meter. After the flow-meter, the oxygen would come to a joint on the instrument board, into which a socket could be pushed, attaching a flexible tube leading to the pilot's and observer's oxygen masks. Metal tubing of a flexible kind was used. If even a drop of moisture froze in a valve, blocking it, fatal consequences might follow, and for that reason the oxygen had to be heated.

The oxygen mask was a somewhat clumsy apparatus. Many straps attached it to the helmet of either the pilot or the observer. It protruded in front, and became entangled with anything in the way, such as the cameras. It fitted over the nose, mouth and chin, had two air holes and a flow of oxygen whose rate depended on the height of the aircraft. At the end of the mask there was a microphone, through which the pilot and observer could talk to each other. This made the oxygen mask even larger. When the microphone was switched on, the ears of the pilot would be filled with crackling. The sound was like a noisy telephone line.

At 30,000 feet pure oxygen would be needed to supplement the rarified air at that altitude. With the oxygen content being only one-third of that at sea-level in the absence of an oxygen mask, it was necessary to oxygenate the blood sufficiently to maintain consciousness. At such a height it was calculated that one man could use six litres of oxygen each minute. If there was any question of not enough oxygen getting through to either the pilot or the observer, each could warn the other on the microphone. If the main oxygen supply operated by the pilot failed, there was a reserve 750-litre cylinder of oxygen, this emergency system being controlled by either the pilot or the observer. If either was in danger of losing consciousness, the other could switch on the reserve supply speedily.

The pilots would have found it much easier with a pressurised cockpit, containing enough oxygen, but this had been ruled out as being too complex, and in any case the observer would have found it hard to handle his cine camera and cameras for taking oblique photographs to the maximum advantage.

Everything had been worked out to the last detail by the time Blacker and Clydesdale went to the Royal Aircraft Establishment at Farnborough, when they had to enter a pressure chamber with a porthole. Clydesdale had noticed that Blacker's monocle had always appeared immoveable. However, inside the chamber, where powerful pumps extracted the air, his monocle fell into his oxygen mask, and it took a considerable effort on his part to replace it without losing too much oxygen.[3] As the air was withdrawn from the chamber, talking became harder and noise less distinct. A sheet of paper dropped would descend like a stone instead of fluttering, there being too little air to delay its fall.

Clydesdale had decided to experiment, to find out what would happen if his oxygen equipment broke down, so that he would know the symptoms of oxygen shortage and would recognise them speedily if there was a crisis. He had been told that at 30,000 feet unconsciousness would follow in about half a minute. When the air had been withdrawn from the chamber to the same extent as it would be at 25,000 feet without oxygen, he removed his oxygen mask. He found that there was a temptation to gasp and it was nearly four minutes before he began to lose consciousness. On replacing the oxygen mask and after a few deep breaths, his full strength returned.

Again when the atmosphere was equivalent to that at 35,000 feet on the altimeter he took off his oxygen mask, and found it very difficult not to gasp. Just after half a minute his sight became affected and he felt he was about to become unconscious. As soon as he replaced the mask with a full supply of oxygen, he recovered.

This experience had two advantages. First he had noticed that several seconds elapsed before unconsciousness due to lack of oxygen follows. Thus a fit pilot, flying at 30,000 feet within reach of level country would have a few seconds to point the aircraft into an appropriate gliding angle, before becoming unconscious. Secondly if a pilot were to become half-conscious near Everest, through lack of oxygen, a few deep breaths could lead to recovery as soon as the emergency supply was switched on. The pilots would have to concentrate on being in training, as the ability to respond quickly in an emergency might be vital.

He and Blacker were conscious of the need to have the best up-to-date meteorological information from the Director of Meteorology in India, Dr. Norman. He agreed to set up balloon stations at Purnea and Darjeeling. By releasing balloons wind direction and speeds up to 35,000 feet could be traced on a clear day. This would enable one or two reports a day on meteorological information to reach the pilots after they arrived at Purnea.[4] This did not alter the fact that such information would constitute a rough general guide, as there might be unknown fierce eddies of wind, including mighty blasts and currents of air rising and falling in the vicinity of Everest. The most that could be discovered would be the wind direction and speeds above Purnea and Darjeeling, and whether there were clouds near Everest.

The Commanding Officer of the Meteorological Flight at Duxford, Flight Lieutenant Pugh, wrote a letter to the press, warning of the dangers:

> At great heights an aeroplane is very unstable and sluggish at the controls and a severe downward current near the mountain would be very dangerous as the aircraft might easily lose many thousands of feet in a matter of seconds.

He went on to say that possible disaster would occur if violent bumps caused structural failure, or if there was engine or magneto stoppage, or a fracture of a fuel pipe, or even a hitch with the oxygen.[5]

The world's press had been following developments with a close interest. It was appreciated that there was no sense of competition between the aviators' expedition and that of the climbers under Hugh Ruttledge. The latter would arrive at Darjeeling for the long march through Tibet towards the end of March, making for the base in the Rongbuk Valley. To conquer Mount Everest in their different ways remained the disinterested aim of both expeditions. In the United States it was reported by the *Mayo News,* Westport:

> These scientific flyers are not overlooking the fact that the slightest miscalculation in their plans spells disaster. The finest aeronautical and meteorological minds have had a hand in their preparations, and the eyes of the entire world will be on them when they set out from India to blaze a new and record breaking air trail over the towering mountain.[6]

Interest in the press had, if anything, been increased by *The Times* acquiring the photographic and newspaper rights to cover the Air Expedition. Mr. Shepherd, the Aviation Editor of *The Times,* was even going to accompany the pilots all the way to India, when the time came, as the official narrator. He wished to tell the story to Europe, America, Asia, Africa and Australia, and he hoped that the Expedition would provide him with the deeds to tell it well.

There were many aspects to the Expedition, but the theme which appealed to the media was that to succeed those involved would require courage to combat the dangers, and none could tell whether they would succeed. The *Nottingham Guardian* wrote:

> To some these venturesome expeditions, such as flying over Everest, or climbing it, or discovering the North or South Pole, seem to involve more dangers than the results are worth. . . . The real justification for these daring ventures lies in the magnificent example of courage they set. We are all potentially braver for Scott's heroic dash to the South Pole and for the glorious assault of Mallory and Irvine on Everest.[7]

There was no doubt that the British press wanted the Air Expedition to succeed. *The Scotsman* wrote: "Success would mean a triumph of British grit and also of British materials, besides resulting in an extension of human knowledge of the planet which we inhabit".[8] There was even public approval for the participation of an M.P.. The *Daily Express* had held a poll for popular young men. Lord Burghley, the Olympic hurdler came top, Clydesdale came tenth, with Randolph Churchill as the spare man.[9] Such approval came in a most direct form from the *Glasgow Weekly Herald's* article about Clydesdale:

> It takes a brave man to take his life in his hands, and go out to meet such dangers. . . . The acme of physical fitness, no thought of failure enters his mind. . . .
>
> In Parliament, his maiden speech was on a subject very close to his heart, aviation. He made a spirited plea for aid, particularly for Scotland and his speech was well received. Since then his voice has not been heard of very often, and within recent months he has not been heard at all, for at a little town in Somerset, Yeovil, he has been preparing for the greatest adventure of his life.[10]

Sure enough at Yeovil at the end of January 1933 Clydesdale was to be found with the intrepid Colonel Blacker. In their high altitude suits, they looked more like figures from outer space than recognisable human beings. In their suits, gloves, helmets and goggles and boots they looked enormous. No part of them was uncovered. Connected to the clothing, gloves, boots and helmets, were electric wires and leads and piping running in many directions, like the wiring in a telephone exchange. Even the eye pieces of the goggles contained electric heating filaments. The electricity was to be provided from dynamos, and if these stopped, the electric current to the clothing would be switched off to allow the small supply from the battery to go to heat the goggles and oxygen, so that the pilot would be able to see and continue flying.

The suits were made of waterproof khaki, lined with kapok, and in between linings of cloth were electric wires, sewn approximately one inch apart, with extra wiring in the knee. The sheepskin boots came up to the calf of the leg and had rubber soles. Between the fleece and the stockinette lining to the boots, electric wires to heat the boots were sewn. The gloves were lined with stockinette with two wires sewn in to heat each finger, gauntlets of leather running over the wrists. The helmets consisted of cloth, the oxygen reaching it through the electrically-heated tube of piping.

Wearing such equipment the first flight in the Houston-Westland was carried out by Harald Penrose, the Westland test pilot, taking Air Commodore Fellowes as a passenger. The temperature at 35,000 feet was minus 60 degrees centigrade. A few days later Clydesdale and Blacker would have their opportunity to test their clothing, oxygen masks, cameras, the generator, the fuel system and the performance of the engine, carrying the necessary weight, as they hoped to stay as long as possible

Air Commodore Fellowes, adjusting Colonel Blacker's heated apparatus

The oxygen chamber to test the pilots' newly designed oxygen equipment

around and over the summit of Mount Everest. In their first climb they found that the highest speed of the Houston Westland was 140 mph at heights over 30,000 feet. Their heating suits and oxygen masks functioned well. The only time that either of them experienced the cold was when Blacker stood up in his opened cockpit to take photographs. The Eagle Survey Camera with its heated cover continued to function at temperatures of minus 71 degrees centigrade.

A week later the Westland Wallace, to be flown by McIntyre, was tested. It had been adapted like the Houston Westland and the test flight nearly led to disaster when the shaft of the petrol pump shattered. The Wallace made a successful forced landing at Hamble, and afterwards it received clearance as being airworthy, less than a week before it was due to be sent out to India by ship, the wings, tail unit and body of the aircraft being packed into a couple of large crates. In February the aeroplanes were loaded, along with a great deal of equipment, on to the *SS Dalgoma* in the London Docks, for the voyage to Karachi.

The participants in the Expedition were assembling their gear, from clothing to rifles and camping requirements, as arrangements had been confirmed with the Royal Air Force and the India Office to use the airstrip at Lalbalu to the East of Purnea and Bihar. The Secretary of the

Harald Penrose, the Westland test pilot

Expedition, Etherton, set off by ship, along with the eight-man film crew of Gaumont British, including the Producer. Blacker made his way out to Karachi by Imperial Airways, leaving six persons to fly out in three small aircraft. Air Commodore Fellowes, with his wife, were to fly out in a Puss Moth. Clydesdale was to fly the Fox Moth intended for transport and reconnaissance, with Shepherd of *The Times* and Hughes, the ground engineer of the Expedition. Finally McIntyre would fly the Gipsy III Moth.

On 16th February 1933, a large gathering assembled at Heston aerodrome to speed the party on its way. Messages of support came from

The Westland Wallace at Yeovil, prepared to fly

The test flight of the Westland Wallace

Colonel Etherton, explorer and secretary of the expedition

Marquis of Clydesdale and Colonel Blacker ready for their first flight

The three Moths with the main party, about to take off from Heston aerodrome for India, 16 February 1933

many sources. King George V had sent his blessing, wishing the pilots every success and saying that he would closely follow developments. Lady Houston too had cabled the Viceroy of India, Lord Willingdon, who had replied that he would give whatever help he could.

Relatives and well-wishers gathered round, and Clydesdale's mother gave him a mascot wrapped up in brown paper to take with him, though she would not say what it was. At last the pilots and the passengers entered their respective aircraft on the grass aerodrome and taxied out, turning off into wind, and soaring up through the light clouds into a sunlit sky. The intense excitement of those moments was recorded later by Fellowes and Clydesdale:

The busy days of preparation were over . . . the propellors had begun the throb and roar and whirl of their ecstatic rush—the swiftest race yet known to man. For a few moments each aeroplane seemed to its neighbour to hover and hang almost motionless as some silver bubble over the irridescent [sic] mist beneath. Only the roar of the engines gave the impression of speed and progress. In the air the infinite always lies ahead and its symbol is the sky.[11]

Left to right: Mr Shepherd, of The Times, *McIntyre, Clydesdale, Air Commodore Fellowes*

4 FLIGHT TO INDIA

THE PILOTS AND organisers of the Expedition had made every conceivable form of preparation, to cover every eventuality, for the flight over Mount Everest. It was not as easy to prepare thoroughly for the journey to India by air, since information as to flying conditions between Britain and India was scanty.

They would have chosen to fly to India through Eastern Europe, but the insurance company concerned would not offer cover unless they travelled to India via France, Italy, Sicily, North Africa and the Middle East. The reason for this was that Balkan aerodromes sometimes became snowbound and waterlogged during winter months. Instead they would have to face the greater risk of gales over the Mediterranean and sandstorms in Africa and the Middle East, to comply with the route laid down by the insurance agents.

The three aircraft which had taken off for Paris were a Gypsy III Moth belonging to Clydesdale, a Puss Moth which was lent by Messrs Fry, the chocolate manufacturers, and a Fox Moth which could be disposed of in India. McIntyre was flying the Gypsy III Moth, and since it was slowest, with a cruising speed of only 90 to 95 miles per hour, it was arranged that he should take the leading position. In an attempt to increase its speed a new Fairey-Reid metal airscrew had been fitted in place of the wooden propeller, and it was further agreed that there should be no passengers in the forward cockpit, which would be covered to make it more streamlined. These modifications had increased the cruising speed by about four miles per hour. Air Commodore Fellowes, with his wife, was flying the Puss Moth and Clydesdale was in charge of the very heavily laden Fox Moth which was intended for transport reconnaissance activities in India.

As well as a great deal of luggage, Clydesdale had accommodated in the aircraft two passengers, Shepherd and Hughes. The Fox Moth had been built in such a way that they were seated in a cabin below and in front of Clydesdale. Just before take off they had been alarmed by a chance comment from a well-wisher that if anything happened to the pilot, it would be impossible for those in the cabin below the cockpit to do anything, as the machine began spinning to earth. Clydesdale noticed that Hughes, who was blue from the cold, looked miserable when confronted with such a thought.[1]

The flight for the 2¾-hour journey to Le Bourget, at a height of 7,000 feet was cold, but a good lunch restored their spirits. Thereafter they flew South towards Lyons, seeing fine snow scattered over the fields. At the outset there were no problems, and they reached Lyons before darkness. Next day, 17th February, they made an early start, arriving at Marseilles not long afterwards. Enquiring about the condition of Italian aerodromes, they learnt that Pisa was not in serviceable condition and Florence was unsuitable. With a range of only 4½ hours in flying time, they took off for Sarzana, a military aerodrome twenty miles from Pisa in North West Italy.

They cruised at 95 miles per hour and flew over the French mountains between Lyons and Nice, making their way along the Riviera coast to Italy, where the low hills resembled the Scottish moors. At Sarzana they were unable to proceed, as it took time to negotiate for the purchase of Italian Air Force petrol. They carried vouchers from the Shell Oil Company, and it was arranged that the bill would be sent to them. By the time refuelling had been completed there was no time to fly on to Rome.

The six members of the Expedition made their way to the local inn, whose owner was appalled at the prospect of having to find beds for so many. It did not help that the pilots and their passengers spoke no Italian, and had to make themselves understood through a combination of French, German and English. They were assisted by a Czech who translated their German into Italian. They were offered three beds among the six of them, beds incidentally which had been slept in during the day by Italians working on nightshift. They were glad to leave the next day, and it was then, on 18th February, that they encountered their first problem.

Mussolini had become Italy's Fascist dictator, claiming that his movement would save his country from Communism. In just over seven years time he would declare war on Britain. In 1933 he was trying to build up Italy's military strength, and the military authorities reacted with suspicion to foreign aircraft flying over Italy, even if they had permission. On leaving Sarzana the Expedition had flown towards Naples, passing over Mount Vesuvius and Pompeii, photographing the crater with its column of smoke. At Naples they were asked if photographs had been taken, and there were looks of stern disapproval when it was admitted that the cameras had been used. They were informed that such aerial photography was completely forbidden. The cameras were taken, the films were extracted, and the cameras were sealed up, so that they could not be used again over Italian territory.[2]

After spending the night of 19th February in Naples, the three aircraft flew South towards Catania in Sicily. On their maps the pilots knew that they must not fly over Messina where they understood that there was a munitions factory, and also over part of the toe of Italy where there were military bases. Between the two districts there was a narrow passage on the map, and both Air Commodore Fellowes in the Puss Moth, and Clydesdale in the Fox Moth flew along this passage. McIntyre, on the other hand, flew to the East some forty miles over the Mediterranean, giving the military areas a wide berth.

After crossing the straits between Italy and Sicily, Clydesdale flew at 10,000 feet over the volcano, Mount Etna, near its snow-covered side, the summit being in dense clouds. He landed at Catania. With Air Commodore Fellowes and McIntyre he was summoned by an Italian Air Force Officer, who announced that the Commandant wished to see the pilots forthwith in the Officers' Mess. There they met the Commandant, with the Chief of the Local Police, who informed them that two of the aircraft had flown over prohibited areas. Interrogation followed, lasting several hours. The Italian Police took the matter very seriously indeed, saying that the British pilots could not be permitted to continue, and certainly not without authority from a very senior source.[3]

The Italian Air Force Officers were much more relaxed and in contrast to the Italian Police, received the British pilots with hospitality and courtesy. At last the Police agreed to allow them to go to a hotel, in exchange for solemn promises that they would not attempt to leave Catania in the absence of permission. At 8 p.m. permission to leave was granted. The Police had evidently come to the conclusion that they were not spying, even if for a long time the British team had not been given the benefit of the doubt. It was now too late to fly on to Tunis that day—their original intention—and their stay at Catania was to be a long one.

On 20th February, the pilots were ready to fly onwards at 7 a.m. but no officials could be found to give them the necessary clearance papers. More than an hour later the papers were received, and the aircraft took off, to be met by thunderstorms which were so heavy that they returned to land at Catania, only be charged an extra landing fee. They again tried to take off later that day, but with no better results. In order to fly over the hills they had to climb up to 4,000 feet and as only one of three aircraft had a turn and bank indicator it was considered injudicious to fly blind in heavy electrical storms.

For the next three days squalls were continual across the mountains. It was difficult to obtain permission to fly on to Trapani on the West coast of Sicily, much nearer Tunis, since it was flooded and was in any case a military aerodrome. Special permission was eventually forthcoming from Rome and on 23rd February, in storms, they flew through the valleys, skirting the worst of the weather in the mountain tops. At Trapani the wind and rain were so great that McIntyre was nearly blown over taxiing the Gipsy III Moth into the hangar, and Clydesdale found that one of the Fox Moth's wheels sank into a soft patch, and the aircraft had to be manhandled out of a bog.

In the hangar the wet and cold pilots and passengers changed into dry clothing, whilst the aircraft were refuelled. They then made their way to what appeared to be the only hotel in Trapani, where the bar was packed with dockside workers and seamen, the other public room being the dining room.

Cold through to the bone, they stared through the windows beyond the harbour, where the muddy waves had white crests, whipped up by the dismal howling of the gale. Here again they found it difficult to be understood without Italian, as the waiter brought no drinks while the party waited for fried eggs. McIntyre was determined that rum should be provided, so that they could shake the cold out of themselves. He approached the waiter, speaking in three languages, drawing a picture of a rum punch bowl, indicating the items which would have to be stirred. The waiter reappeared with lemon, hot water and sugar, but still no rum, although he did offer whisky.

Sign language had not been enough, but it was not easy to put off McIntyre. He looked over the bottles in the bar, and, finding no rum, looked at the sailors. The thought occurred to him that for sailors hornpipes and rum had a clear relationship. Attracting the attention of the waiter, he performed a hornpipe. The sailors and Italian workers found this very entertaining, and a smile spread across the waiter's face. A rum bottle appeared, with only a little in it, sufficient for one issue of rum punch to the pilots and their passengers. Thus it was that they restored their own health, and drank to the health of McIntyre, at a huge meal of eggs with bread, sprinkled with aniseeds. After that they sought their beds.[4]

By 7.30 a.m. on 24th February they were ready to take off from Trapani aerodrome for Tunis, but the storm continued. They were warned with dreadful tales. Signorina Angelica had left in an aeroplane on a day when the weather was as bad, and she had never landed in Africa, coming down in the sea. There had as well been an Italian Count who had taken off and had disappeared forever. After six hours of waiting there was a break in the weather and they dallied no longer, their aircraft taking off into a strong wind. Skirting a large thunder cloud, they made the 150-mile crossing to

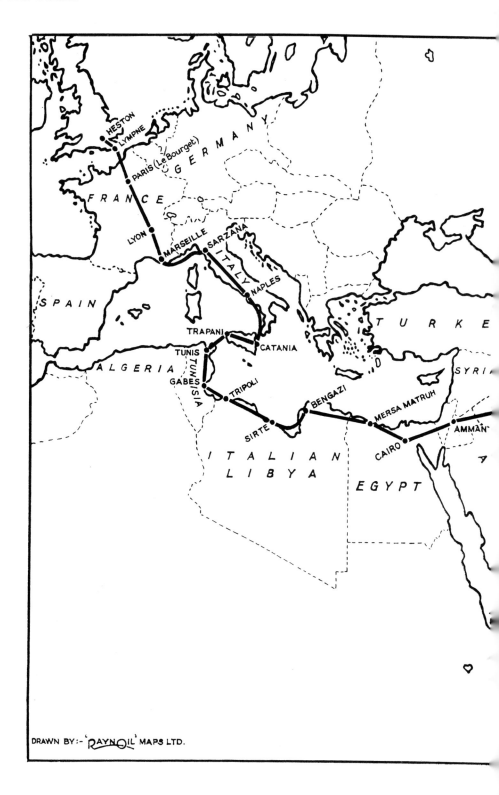

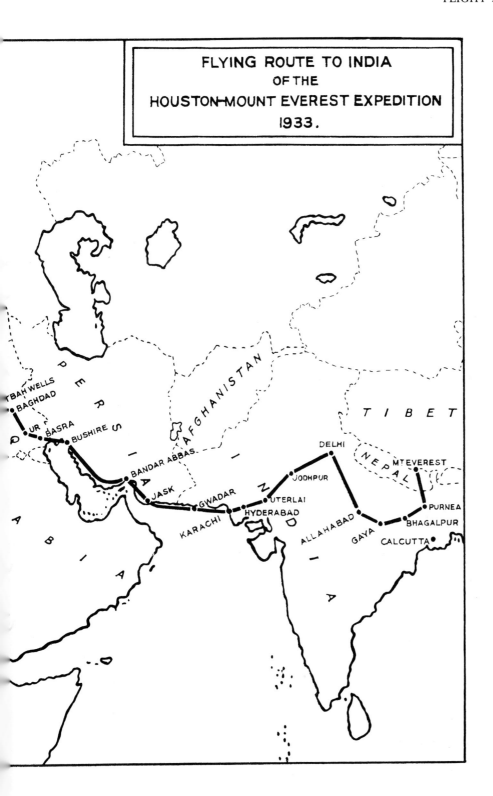

FLYING ROUTE TO INDIA
OF THE
HOUSTON-MOUNT EVEREST EXPEDITION
1933.

Tunisia in two-and-half-hours. They only saw two ships, and it occurred to them that if an engine had stopped, bringing down an aircraft in the sea, it might have been a very long time before a ship came past.

On landing they had a very different reception from the one experienced at Catania. The local Shell representative introduced the party to officers from the African Aviation Group, whose commanding officer gave the six visitors warm but formal French hospitality in the Air Force Mess. There were speeches and with champagne the friendship between Britain and France was celebrated.

The sun was shining and they travelled into Tunis, finding the colour and warmth of North Africa a welcome change after the stormy conditions of Trapani. They passed a flock of flamingos, catching a glimpse of the site of Carthage in the distance. They realised that they had left the wintry conditions of Europe behind and now faced the challenge of making their way across the desert.

Next day the pilots considered the prospect of flying from Tunis to Tripoli, and took off early in the morning, flying into a headwind. When they reached the small French town of Gabes, in the midst of a featureless desert, they decided to land and refuel. They had to obtain the petrol from the town in a horse gharry, and by 1 o'clock they had arrived in Tripoli of Italian Libya. By evening they had flown another 300 miles to El Sirte in the blazing heat of the sun. There, when the pilots and passengers asked the way to the local rest house, the Italian officers replied that it was out of the question for them to consider it, and invited them to a good dinner with accommodation.

In the morning, on 26th February, they were again ready by first light, and at dawn they laid course for the next stage, eating a hard boiled egg and a lump of aniseed bread which Mrs. Fellowes had taken with her from Trapani, in case it should be needed in place of breakfast. They landed at Benghazi, where the high wind was blowing dustclouds across the aerodrome. A throw-away comment by McIntyre on the nature of their breakfast in mid-air led to the Italian officers offering them a second breakfast of coffee and toast, fried eggs and even fruit and wine. This would serve as lunch as well.

While there they became concerned about the existence of 40 mph howling winds but were reassured that such winds did not exist above 3,000 feet. Air Commodore Fellowes therefore recommended flying at this height or above. McIntyre, on the other hand, had found it warmer to fly at lower levels, rather than grow very cold from flying seven to eight hours a day in an open cockpit.

They flew on to Tobruk and McIntyre's navigation proved to be extremely accurate, in spite of the crosswinds. Flying the slowest machine, McIntyre went first, and over the desert he had to follow a compass course over land where there was no long grass or smoke to show the direction of the wind. In Tobruk the aircraft were refuelled rapidly. The Italian Commanding Officers offered refreshments in the aerodrome, and within

45 minutes the three aircraft were again airborne. Soon they were across the Egyptian frontier, and paused over El Sollum, but resolved to do everything possible to press on to Mersa Matruh that night. It was a calculated risk, and they arrived only five minutes before darkness. The pilots "watched the black band of night advancing across the desert from the East. It was an uncomfortable sensation, sitting up there at 3,000 feet and trying to calculate whether the darkness or the aeroplane would be the first to reach the landing ground about midway between them. It was just as well that we won. The small unlighted aerodrome could never have been found in the dark, and with its bad surface and the rough country round it, something would probably have been broken in landing."[5]

The Pyramids photographed from the air at Cairo

In Mersa Matruh they were glad to reach a good hotel. Only Shepherd was disappointed, since the telegraphs and telephones were not operational after 6 p.m.. *The Times* of London would have to wait for an up to date account. Next day they were off again, flying over the Pyramids and landing at Almaza to stay two days in Cairo, while the engines of the aircraft were checked and inspected. The Royal Air Force officers in Cairo gave them an especial welcome, since one of the Expedition's purposes was to establish the worth of British machinery.

Two days later they again took off, seeing little of the ground as a sand storm obscured much of Egypt. They flew over Palestine, the Dead Sea, Jerusalem and Jericho and landed at Amman in TransJordan. That evening they were told that eighteen criminals and convicted murderers from the prison in A Wadi near the Royal Air Force base had escaped, after overcoming the guards and stealing their arms. Just before they went to sleep they received two pieces of information. The first was a relief in that twelve of the prisoners had been recaptured, but the second was the meteorological report which indicated that they would be well advised to make an early start the next day as more dust storms between Amman and the 500-mile stretch to Baghdad in Iraq were expected.

After the First World War Air Commodore Fellowes had been involved in establishing a furrow, made by a plough, so that aircraft could be guided by it to Baghdad. Alongside it an oil pipeline had been constructed into a dust road. Following these turned out to be harder than anticipated. After taking off from Amman they followed the pipeline closely, and in the poor visibility as the whirling sandstorm became more dense the three aircraft became separated, losing sight of each other. Buried in cloud and flying low over land hard to distinguish from the sand-filled air, flying was a frightening pastime.

Clydesdale with the Fox Moth was the first to reach the landing strip at Rutbah Wells in Iraq, at 9.40 a.m.. The other two aircraft had not yet arrived, since they missed the point at which they should have left the pipeline and had to fly back to find it. McIntyre appeared at Rutbah Wells some ten minutes later, and the Air Commodore found his way there half-an-hour after that, as he had flown further and had to retrace his tracks.

On the ground at Rutbah Wells the pilots could see little on account of the dust storms of choking yellow dust. Having learned that for much of the way between there and Baghdad, visibility was not more than five yards, they settled in the rest house. They were impressed by the nature of the fort there and by the strict observance of the Muslim religion, with evening prayers for many pilgrims who arrived in cars, on their way to the shrine of Mecca. The law, too, appeared to be strictly upheld when armed police appeared in vehicles loaded with prisoners who had been charged with stealing hundreds of sheep. The members of the Expedition remained at the rest house, grateful to eat and drink, in the knowledge that all provisions had been ferried 250 miles for the travellers who came there.

On 3rd March they were up after 5 a.m. and saw that the raging winds had subsided. The aircraft soared into the air and, after finding the pipeline again, followed the sunrise in the direction of Baghdad. They saw camels eating the scrub and rough grass, and as daylight approached they could see the track bearing occasional cars. Within two hours they spotted the river Euphrates. They reached Baghdad by breakfast time.

They had hoped to go on to Persia speedily,but the British Ambassador and Iraqi officials could not discover the visas which the Indian Government had been requested to grant. This gave them the opportunity to see Baghdad and, in one case, to visit the brother of an old friend. Clydesdale had befriended HRH the Emir Deid at Balliol College, Oxford, the Emir being the brother of King Feisal of Iraq. The Emir Deid had surprised him at Oxford by offering him a revolver. Apparently he had produced the gun in front of his tutor during a tutorial, and his tutor had told him that he must give it away. By this no doubt he meant that he should hand it over to someone for safekeeping. Clydesdale had been reticent about accepting such a gift, and the Emir Deid had made it clear that he would be offended if it was not accepted. The revolver ended up in Clydesdale's father's locked safe.

King Feisal, being aware of Clydesdale's friendship with his brother, gave him an audience, and showed a readiness to appreciate the importance of air supremacy for maintaining law and order in his country. He asked many question about the plans to fly over Everest and about the need for oxygen masks. He was developing his own Air Force, and felt that modern aircraft would greatly hasten the speed of communications in his country.[6]

The pilot and the other members of the Expedition later visited Baghdad, which they found to be a centre of commerce. Some of their most vivid memories were of odours of garlic and of oil, the fuel in a land with few trees, and the principal source of wealth. On returning to the British Embassy they expressed anxiety to proceed to Karachi, so that they could be there when the two larger aircraft were to be assembled.

By 4th March they had received their permits, but the weather again took a change for the worse with dust storms. The experts on meteorology considered that Basra would be clear. The Expedition thus made its way southwards, flying, as advised by the Royal Air Force, along a railway line. Before two hours had elapsed the air was so dense with dust and visibility so poor that they could only see the railway when flying as low as 100 feet above. After groping their way for another half an hour, they decided to touch down beside a railway station, by way of forced landings on a stretch of level ground. There they found themselves at Batha Station, whose Stationmaster had enough English to advise them to follow the railway for some 20 miles to a small landing area at Ur.

There was no sign of the Air Commodore at this stage for he had flown out of the sandstorm and on to Shaibah. McIntyre and Clydesdale discussed the risks and McIntyre offered to fly to Ur, and telegraph back if the conditions were acceptable. Since Clydesdale had two passengers, one of whom was unwell (Hughes, who was unaccustomed to Iraqi food), this offer was accepted. Meanwhile telegrams were sent by Clydesdale to Hinaidi and Shaiba, in case Air Commodore Fellowes had got through safely, and to let him know about the forced landings.

After half an hour a message was received from McIntyre that he had landed safely, and Clydesdale flew down the railway line, with visibility about 500 yards. Without difficulty he found McIntyre signalling in the middle of the landing strip. They went to the railway rest house at Ur, where they received the good news from the Air Commodore that he had reached Shaiba in safety and that he was dispatching fuel on the train for them. On checking they found out that they had enough fuel, and the next day the two aircraft were airborne before the train came. They arrived in Shaiba even before the Air Commodore was awake on 5th March.

Shortly after 9 a.m. that day the three aircraft proceeded towards Iran, over the mud flats near the estuary of the Tigris, past the refinery at Abadan with its numerous oil tanks and its large flame burning the excess gases. At midday they landed at the Persian aerodrome of Bushire and for the first time for days touched down on a grass runway, with even signs of trees and flowers—a refreshing sight. The other surprise was that the weather proved to be very cold in comparison to the other parts of the Middle East they had visited.

The Persian permits were well enough ordered, identifying the aircraft and occupants, but for some unknown reason McIntyre's name had been omitted. The vigorous activities of Captain Gastrell, the British Assistant Resident at Bushire, soon helped to resolve this matter. Furthermore, Shepherd was able to cable *The Times,* and such was the reputation of the newspaper there, he did not even have to pay for it in Persian money. If he said that *The Times* would pay for it on delivery, then without question it was accepted that it would be done.[7]

Early on 6th March they left Bushire, seeing "the sun climb up red and gold from behind the clouds on the mountain tops."[8] As soon as they had taken off, they skirted around the bases of mountains coming down to the sea, in the shape of jagged teeth, leaving only a strip of steep beach if their aircraft met with any emergencies. They found this country as beautiful and impressive as it was daunting. With a wind behind them they soon arrived at Bandar Abbas, further South in Iran. There they found the heat to be considerable and began to wear their topees. Fuel was carried on the backs of donkeys to the aircraft, and in order to make sure that no dust got into the petrol tanks, the pilots climbed on the wings, pouring tin after tin of petrol into the tanks through the handkerchiefs they used for straining. The officials there, however, were not impressed by the clearance received at Bushire. They searched the aircraft for smuggled goods, inspected the cameras and passports, insisting on health certificates. The negotiations were left to Air Commodore Fellowes. He bluffed with them, changed the conversation, and gave them a mass of statistics about horsepower, load and tankage of the aircraft. But even his calm manner nearly evaporated when he was asked how many rats he was carrying on board.

As they prepared to take off, the handkerchief which had been used to strain petrol by Clydesdale was blown into the control cables near the tail. After lift-off he realised that this was the cause of the elevator control being stiff, and he made a landing on sand to extract it. He again took off into a crosswind, and the aircraft, after going over a sandy bump, lurched into the air before it had achieved full flying speed. For a moment Clydesdale did not dare ease the stick forward or backward in case the wheels of the aircraft touched again, wiping off the undercarriage. Gradually the speed increased and the aircraft with its two passengers joined up with the rest of the Expedition.

In view of their experience with the officials at Bandar Abbas, the pilots pressed on for India, hoping to reach Gwadar in Baluchistan. The rock formations from the air seemed to take on the form of towers, fortifications and cathedrals, but on a closer look they were "only strange rock shapes, cut by the tropical storms of centuries, and fretted by the sand-laden winds".[9] As evening fell, they landed at Gwadar, having travelled 850 miles that day.

Since morning they had had neither food nor drink, and at Gwadar landing strip they were some eight miles from the town. Near the aerodrome were wells, but they resisted the temptation, as none of them wished to contract illness through drinking from untreated water. There was no proper road to Gwadar, but at the rest hut there was a telephone, and the Gwadar Post Office was contacted. The members of the Expedition promised the official there that his Bank Account in the Bank of India at Karachi would be credited if food could be conveyed to them. They were deeply moved to realise that they had been trusted implicitly by

Unloading the Westland Wallace at Karachi

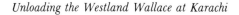

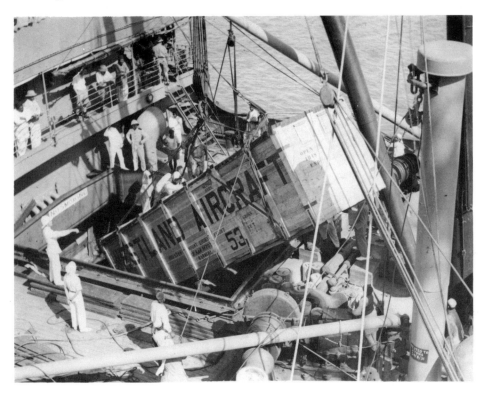

Assembling the Wallace at Karachi

the man and they were to recall this as a highlight in the many acts of kindness accorded them on their way to India. There appeared before them on heavily laden donkeys and camels a cook with his assistant, food, beer, mineral water, and bedding for the night. They quenched their burning thirst.

Apart from Mrs. Fellowes, who slept in the Puss Moth, they slept out in the open, forgetting that the early morning hours might bring with them a heavy dew. When Clydesdale woke up that morning of 7th March his jacket and trousers were soaked with water. He refuelled the aircraft in his pyjamas, his clothes flapping on the bracing wires of the aeroplane. McIntyre, on the other hand, had slept on planks under a tarpaulin and did not have to rely on the sun to dry his clothes.

Having worked out on the calculator the time it would take to cover the 300 miles to Karachi, they estimated the flight time to be three hours. Soon they took off and arrived there in plenty of time to have lunch in the luxurious surroundings of the Sind Club.

Their trip had fascinated them in spite of its anxieties. It had taken two weeks and four days to reach India with three aircraft intact and no casualties. They had been supported fully by British Embassies in each country, as well as by the Royal Air Force in lands under British administration. Now they would have to journey across India to their base camp to complete the final preparations for their assault on the world's greatest and most inaccessible mountain.

5 GLIMPSES OF EMPIRE

AT KARACHI THE pilots were settled into the sumptious surroundings of the Sind Club, where they found themselves being looked after by a large number of Indians. Blacker had arrived there, days before them, having travelled out with Imperial Airways. He had given an interview to the *Air and Airways* magazine, summarising the up to date aims of the Expedition:

First from the viewpoint of national prestige, we hope to demonstrate that a standard British aircraft, after only a few structural alterations, is capable of traversing any mountain in the world, carrying its normal full load.

Secondly the Expedition proposes to carry out a careful investigation of the uncharted air currents that constantly swirl above and around the Summit of Mount Everest, and it is also hoped to bring back information which may be of value to meteorological science.

Finally by means of aerial photography, an accurate survey will be attempted of the hitherto unexplored regions close to Everest—a task which, if carried out on foot, would entail months or possibly years of hard work, even were the summit to prove accessible to ground parties.[1]

On arrival at Karachi he had made arrangements with the Royal Air Force Depot for the erection, inspection and testing of the two Westland aircraft, once they had been unloaded off crates from the *SS Dalgoma.* So confident was he that arrangements were in hand that he made his way by train to Delhi where the R.A.F. again offered every assistance. He travelled on by rail and by paddle steamer down the Ganges and by rail again until he was within twenty miles motoring distance of Purnea. He reached the small town by car, and found that Came, the Executive Engineer of the Public Works Department had been hard at work. The landing ground at Lalbalu was being prepared with canvas hangers for the Westland aircraft. The Police Department had been keeping an eye on proceedings, as indeed had the Commissioner of the Province.

Meanwhile Air Commodore Fellowes decided that it would be advisable for Clydesdale and McIntyre to use the air route across India which they would have to make with the Westland, so that no unnecessary risks would be taken. In any case the unloading of the two Westlands looked as if it would take some time, since they had to be transported nine miles from the dock by rail to the Royal Air Force Depot. It was on this journey that the two pilots had many glimpses of the Indian Empire from land and air.

For almost two days Clydesdale and McIntyre were not airborne and they felt refreshed when they flew to Hyderabad, Uterlai and Jodhpur on 9th March. Much concentration was required as considerable distances were involved, the landmarks being relatively few. That night the Maharajah of Jodhpur, who was very interested in flying and had his own aerodrome and his own aircraft, asked the two pilots to stay as his guests. They visited his Palace, perched on a hill with extensive fortifications. By the entrance they noticed numerous handprints of silver on the stone at the gate, revealing the custom of suttee which Hindu wives had followed in past centuries. Apparently when a Prince died, his wives would leave the print of their hands at the gate before immolating themselves in the flames of their husband's funeral pyre. Even the pilots were taken aback with awe at the extent of such devotion and sacrifice. They were also introduced to the existence of purdah, under which Indian ladies wore the veil so that their faces would not be seen in public. The pilots noticed that there was a purdah room in the Palace, from which the Maharanee might see the aerodrome, while remaining invisible herself.

On 10th March they flew on to Delhi, where they met Blacker, then together the three of them flew past Cawnpore, Allahabad and Benares, reaching Gaya the next day. On their way they had their first sight of Mount Everest. It moved Blacker deeply:

> Suddenly, up from out of the hard straight line where the haze met the azure basin of the sky, there appeared three wondrous points of white.
> Over our right wings we saw, wreathed in clouds, that which was Kanchenjunga, and ahead there enthralled our gaze, the far distant crests of Everest and Makalu.

Jodhpur aerodrome with the fleet of Rolls Royces beside the hangar

Three immaculate snowy pinnacles swam majestically alone over this wine-dark sea of mist. We could scarcely bear to glide down to land, and so to lose the beauty of this sight, even for an hour.[2]

They continued from Gaya to Bhagalpur, where Etherton was occupied with the organising of supplies and all four of them flew on to Purnea, and touched down at Lalbalu, where the landing ground was in good order. The canvas hangars were being pitched, and countless Indian labourers were assisting. They then flew North towards Nepal, looking for the emergency landing strip at Forbesgangj in case their aircraft ran out of fuel on its return journey from Everest. A decision was made to level the ground, mark it and leave some fuel there. Being sure that everything was in order they returned to Lalbalu, where they left the Gypsy Moth in a canvas hangar. Then they flew back to Bhagalpur, to be welcomed by the British Commissioner late on 11th March.

Here Etherton parted ways with the other three, as he had received a rare invitation to visit the Maharajah of Nepal in the capital Kathmandu, and to attend Coronation celebrations. Even if the Kingdom of Nepal had sent 80,000 Gurkhas to fight with the British in the First World War, Nepal and indeed neighbouring Tibet, were forbidden countries to almost all Europeans. Under the King, the Maharaja, Sir Joodha Shum Shere Jung Bahadur Rana was the Supreme Commander-in-Chief and the Prime Minister of Nepal, having become Maharaja of Nepal in September 1932. An invitation from him was a unique event, and Etherton accepted at once. He was always aware that the presence of aircraft over Nepal might cause alarm and would give reassurances that they would fly high enough not to alarm anyone. In fact even though the aircraft did not propose to fly over Tibet, Etherton still had to reassure the Dalai Lama, for there had been rumours amongst the Nepalese and Tibetans that Mallory and Irvine had been hurled to their deaths on Mount Everest for having disturbed the Home of the Gods and arousing their wrath.

In these circumstances Etherton was anxious to allay fears and suspicions, and if possible to obtain permission for the Expedition to undertake a second flight. In case there was any difficulty with planning during the first flight, and to obtain the scientific knowledge they required for mapping, it had been recognised early on, that a second flight might well be essential.

He set off for Nepal by railway, and rested at the bungalow in Sisagarhi, which the Maharajah provided for his guests. When he came to Kathmandu he stayed with Colonel Daukes at the British Legation, who had kept the Maharajah informed of the progress of the Expedition and its scientific aims. Together they went to the Maharajah's Palace, to be met by a guard of honour and the Maharajah, who was as welcoming as he was courteous. Going up the staircase he pointed to a painting of the shoot in Nepal in which King George V had taken part in 1911. They proceeded to a drawing room for a general discussion, and then to Etherton's delight the Maharajah agreed to the proposals to have a second flight to Everest if necessary. He specified certain conditions. There were to be no practice flights over Nepal; he must receive a warning of the intention to fly over Nepal; and there must be no general photography of Nepal other than that associated with the air survey of the area around Mount Everest.

Etherton explained that the timing of the flights would depend on

Nepal Government Railway Engine at Raxaul Station

The Maharajah of Nepal

weather conditions and that the Maharajah would receive reports very soon after any flight. The Maharajah stated his preference for being informed beforehand, receiving the official reports immediately thereafter. Etherton gave him an undertaking that he would send a full report once the flight was completed, and at that stage would set out the reasons for a second flight if it was necessary. He was left with the impression that the Maharajah was an enlightened man, ready to keep abreast of modern developments, and that he would give permission for a second flight if any photography was unfinished.

He received a further invitation from the Maharajah to attend the review of the Nepalese Army, where he watched 30,000 men, mostly infantrymen with some light artillery, march past in perfect formation, dressed identically to the British Army in India and formed on the British model. It was a most impressive force, and confirmed for Etherton an understanding of the mutual admiration and respect that had existed for more than a century between Britain and the land of the Gurkhas.[3]

With his good news Etherton hastened to Delhi only to learn that the others had experienced a setback. On 12th March, Clydesdale, McIntyre and Blacker flew back towards Karachi, reaching Allahabad, almost halfway to Delhi. There the Fox Moth was tied down with ropes from blocks of cement, buried in the ground for mooring aircraft. After darkness a tropical storm had hit Allahabad with ferocious force. Trees were wrenched out, houses were destroyed and the hurricane tore the Fox Moth away, blew it a hundred yards overturned it and left it upside down and broken. In the darkness only the flashes of lighting enlightened Clydesdale as to its fate. He watched it with the same emotion a Captain has when his ship begins to sink. With Blacker and McIntyre the wreckage was tied down.

The next day they assessed the seriousness of this setback. The Fox Moth had carried food, luggage, equipment in great quantities, and two or three passengers apart from the pilot.[4] Being 1,100 miles from Karachi, they turned, with a sense of humiliation to the hot and dusty travel by train to Delhi, a journey which only reinforced their enthusiasm for the air. They had been pleasantly surprised flying across India to see that the Shell Oil Company had organised cans of petrol all the way across the country to Purnea for the larger Westland aircraft, and longed to get back to Karachi so that they could be flown to the Base Camp.

In Delhi Clydesdale and Blacker managed to obtain a lift towards Karachi in a Puss Moth, and McIntyre tucked himself into the aircraft cabin full of mailbags of the Royal Indian Air Mail, bound for Karachi as well. Once there, they began a course of physical training. They played football, swam and went for runs, as well as making themselves intimately acquainted with their Westland aircraft, which were being assembled at the R.A.F. Depot. They had a close relationship with the R.A.F. Officers there.

In their spare time away from work, Clydesdale and McIntyre were introduced to the excitement of surf-bathing at the island of Manora. They enjoyed this sport, in which they soon became skilled, picking up bruises and grazing as soon as they allowed the breakers to carry them on to the shore. They also saw at first hand the ingenuity of the kitehawks, when a Squadron Leader carrying a large plate of ham, chicken, potato salad and salad with tomato found himself without his lunch. A kite had dived down out of formation, sweeping away the food in its talons. It remained gliding in the air, eating up the contents between its talons, the rest of the party looking on with amusement at this aerial brigand's impudence and daring.

The R.A.F. Officers gave Clydesdale and McIntyre a great deal of help by sharing with them the benefit of their past experiences of flying in India. They assembled the Westland aircraft and took much trouble to do it well, preparing them for the flight across India.[5] This support given by the R.A.F. was crucial. With Clydesdale and McIntyre as Officers in the Royal Auxiliary Air Force, the Regular Officers understood that if the Expedition succeeded it could help British Aeronautical Companies to play a leading role in world aviation.

The R.A.F. had agreed to provide personnel to maintain and service the

The devastated Fox Moth after the hurricane

The Prime Minister of Nepal at the Military Review

The holy man of Nepal blessing the flight

Clydesdale in the cockpit with Richard Ellison the reserve RAF pilot

Westland aircraft, once they were ready, to provide ground equipment in the form of tents, and to lend the services of a Reserve Regular R.A.F. pilot, Flying Officer Dick Ellison, who was energetic and efficient and who had a very high reputation as a pilot. He and the other officers at the depot were familar with the Jupiter engine and were glad to be involved.

Flying Officer Ellison had been extremely pleased to be invited, all the more so, since a more senior R.A.F. officer had arrived in Karachi saying that he had been sent out from Britain for the special purpose of being Reserve pilot to the Expedition. On the same evening Ellison had received a telegram from the Air Officer commanding in India, asking him to participate as the Reserve pilot and he had accepted.

It occurred to him that with their Pegasus engines the Houston-Westland PV3 and the Wallace were the only ones of their kind in India. The Pegasus engine was so advanced in comparison to the Jupiter engine that those at the Depot wished to examine closely the new engines.

Within three days of arrival the Wallace was ready for flight. The Houston Westland was ready a short time later. The test flights were regarded by the pilots as being of great importance. They had to be sure that they were used to flying with the new engine, and to taking off and landing without damaging the large propellor and airscrew which revolved very close to the ground before take-off or landing. They needed enough practice of high altitude flying to know how to react in any kind of emergency and to become familiar with all the numerous gadgets and controls in the cockpit.

At the same time the Expedition grew into a much bigger party, through the appearance of the film unit under the direction of the celebrated film director, Geoffrey Barkas. He had acted as Director for several films, including "*Tell England*" with Anthony Asquith. Absorbed in his task he turned out to be demanding and programmes had to be rearranged to meet the needs for filming. The two Westland aircraft were filmed in great detail, as were the pilots, even when climbing in and out of their heated flying suits. Geoffrey Barkas had obtained a Ford lorry and it had been converted into a mobile sound unit, ready to record wherever work was in hand. Some six skilled assistants and a great many Indians accompanied him. One of these assistants was the cinematographer, who, it had already been decided, would fly with McIntyre on the first flight over Mount Everest.

On 15th March, McIntyre, with Bonnett, made a high altitude test flight in the Wallace and flew up to the height of 34,000 feet. He made the climb in an hour and a half and was able to see 40 miles through the dust haze, the survey camera and the oxygen masks operating effectively, in a temperature of minus 45 degrees centigrade. At such a height he felt that the summit of Everest might be cleared by about 5,000. The only misfortune was Bonnett's unpleasant experience. He was wearing shorts in the heat of Karachi and his knees were scorched by the electrically heated suit. Kneeling down to open the hatch for the purpose of photography the heating elements in his suit had burnt him. He had then switched off the heating, and become victim of the cold.

The day afterwards Clydesdale and Blacker took up the Houston-Westland PV3. The weather was extremely hot and visibility was excellent. Clydesdale made a slow and steady climb, allowing the aircraft to gain sufficient height as well as to travel the 160 miles from their future base camp at Purnea to Mount Everest. It took him two hours and fifteen minutes to reach 35,000 feet where they could see approximately 150 miles to the East. To the West there were clouds.

The only complication was that the heating of one glass of Clydesdale's goggles and one of Blacker's had failed, frosting over the lens. Blacker also burnt his knees as Bonnett had before him. But with the pilot and observer each having one good eye, the necessary photographs were taken, their descent taking 45 minutes at the end of their three-hour flight. This was the first full dress rehearsal for flying over Mount Everest. Apart from minor adjustments, the two aircraft had responded well, and it was resolved to move on to Purnea. McIntyre recorded that they were eating, drinking and sleeping with Mount Everest uppermost in their minds.

The two large aircraft required leaded petrol and fuel, and it was advisable that there should be supplies at every aerodrome across India. In this connection the Royal Air Force pilot, Dick Ellison, came to the

Left to right: Blacker, Clydesdale and Fellowes, planning the route to Everest

assistance of the Expedition. The R.A.F. had nominated him as a reserve pilot, and after the loss of the Fox Moth, the Karachi Flying Club agreed to lend their most ancient aircraft. He would fly it with Mr. Gallimore of the Burmah Shell Company, who could mix the special leaded fuel with the necessary expertise. This old aircraft had a top speed of 75 mph and its range was not long, causing it to land more often than the two modern aircraft. Ellison would go on ahead in it with the fuel, to be followed by the Houston Westland PV3 and by the Houston Wallace shortly thereafter.

The pilots had been told repeatedly by Air Commodore Fellowes to do all their thinking on the ground, so that they could be prepared for every eventuality, including the most unlikely emergencies, in the air. They had to know what to do and be certain that they would do it automatically. They tested each other on their reactions and knowledge, and on how to decide on the best course of action in any one of a vast variety of adverse circumstance. They watched their instruments closely, so that their reactions would be very rapid.

Sergeant Greenwood was in charge of the R.A.F. Party, keeping an eye on all their equipment. Corporal Bradley was an experienced electrician who looked after the electrical gear, and he was in fact responsible for adapting the flying suits to eliminate the scorching from heating elements in the knee. He tested all the electrical equipment after each flight. Aircraftman Fraser kept the cameras in good working order, fitting the

Survey Cameras after loading them into the aircraft. Aircraftman Clark watched over the airscrews. Aircraftman Hensley was responsible for replacing any fabric, checking the fittings and rigging, as well as special instruments. Last but not least Aircraftman Young guarded the oxygen cylinders and the oxygen system, which would be the lifeline of the pilots and their observers.[6]

The R.A.F. was determined that, if at all possible, the Expedition would succeed. The Puss Moth departed on the 20th March, flown by Air Commodore Fellowes, carrying Mrs. Fellowes and Shepherd as passengers. The larger aircraft were flown by Clydesdale and McIntyre, and they took much luggage and in Clydesdale's case an observer and a mechanic in a separate cockpit in front and below the pilot.

They took off through a soft mist into a cloudless sky, passing over many creeks along the shore, and they caught sight of what was in fact the largest building in the world. It was a hangar designed to accommodate the giant airships, the R100 and the R101. Fellowes had been involved with their building as the Director of Airship Development, but had become Director of Personal Services at the Air Ministry when the R101 crashed on the ridge of Beauvais in France in 1930. It had been on its way to India to this very hangar, which now accommodated instead two football fields for troops, well shaded from the overpowering rays of the sun. The fate of the R101 with the loss of many senior R.A.F. officers had led to the breaking up of the R100 and the abandonment of airship development. The members of the Expedition now looked down at the vast building with a sense of dread. It represented an aspect of the British Aviation Industry which had come to grief.

The hangar constructed to house the R101, which crashed on its way out to India

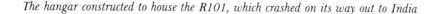

Hyderabad from the Houston Westland

Soon the coastal outline and the sea faded away as they flew over the yellow plains of the Sind Desert. They landed at Hyderabad near the Indus river where a large fascinated crowd had gathered at the aerodrome, bringing home to them that there was much interest in India in their Expedition.

Gallimore and Ellison had left the specially mixed fuel, which was poured into the petrol tanks, and they were away again. The country they flew over had some scrub and small groups of hills, and the observers had their opportunity to photograph when the aircraft reached the fortress of Jodhpur, overlooking the town. There, the Maharajah was away and he had asked his relative Thakur Narbat Singh to entertain the British party. A squadron of Rolls Royce cars picked up their guests, to be taken to the Palace for lunch. They were shown their bedrooms, which were modern and luxurious, and in the evening they went down into the town. The population appeared relatively wealthy, in spite of the crowded living conditions and the swarms of flies which hovered over the food in the market place. The visitors drove back to the new stone Palace, which was half-finished, and were later given a magnificent dinner[7] in the old Palace.

On 21st March they made for Delhi, as the members of the Expedition wished to thank the Viceroy, Lord Willingdon, for his moral and practical support. His influence had led many Maharajahs to become interested in aviation. As they flew, they saw villages and towns tucked into the Indian plains and in the north some rugged hills. Approaching Delhi, they could

The view of Imperial Delhi from the air

The Viceroy Lord Willingdon with Blacker

appreciate its amazing contrasts. It was the most striking city they had seen in all India, and the mosques, including that of Jammu Masjid and its monuments, were in contrast to the planned structure and modern buildings of New Delhi. But there was yet another view of Delhi, of many buildings huddled together, almost as though they would give protection to each other.

That afternoon the Viceroy personally inspected the aircraft at the aerodrome, then he along with the Commander-in-Chief of British Armed Forces in India, Sir Philip Chetwode, offered the members of the Expedition generous hospitality. That night the Viceroy asked Blacker to stay, the Director of Civil Aviation invited the Air Commodore and his wife, and the Commander-in-Chief put up Clydesdale.

Early on the 22nd March, the aircraft flew onwards. The Air Commodore flew over the Taj Mahal, so that his wife could photograph it. As they approached Allahabad they could see the Ganges sweep away in the direction of Calcutta and the sea. The brown waters of the great river were slow moving, and they knew that no river in the world was regarded as being more holy to many millions of Hindus and pilgrims. Here as well there was a direct connection with Everest and the Himalayas, since the waters of the Ganges descended from these mountains. Not only would the aviators have to pursue their mission with dedication, they would also have to treat Everest with the respect accorded to a great natural shrine.

Waiting for lunch at the aerodrome at Allahabad they wandered through the mango groves, watching the oxen sheltering in a muddy pool. They saw an aircraft arrive with three engines, a sight which reminded them that with only one engine on their large aircraft, there was no scope for taking any unnecessary risks.

They were irritated by the vast swarms of flies, and were glad to get back into the aircraft and set course for Purnea. As they came in to land at the Lalbalu airstrip Clydesdale's thoughts were on the countryside, in case he should ever have to make a forced landing. The fields were brown, interspersed with streams, patches of bog, trees and grass. The roads were straight and white, fringed with trees, and two rivers were winding around the fertile countryside.

It was in this area that their base was to be, only an hour and a half's flying time from the summit of Everest and the mountains they had come to challenge. They landed and were driven to Darbhanga bungalow where they would stay, and on some nine miles east of it to the aerodrome at Lalbalu which had a small landing strip. They hoped that they would be joined shortly by the mechanics and film team, who were travelling more slowly across India by train to Darbhanga.

Ellison had arrived at Lalbalu earlier in the ancient aircraft lent to the Expedition, and word had spread amongst the local population. Many thousands of Indians had appeared and spread themselves across the length and breadth of the small landing strip. As he could not land without running into many of the local population he flew round again circling, in the hope that the runway would clear. It did not. The fascination was so great that the crowd stood watching.

He dived towards the landing strip again and again, causing the Indians to scatter, until he had a large enough clear path to attempt a landing. As soon as he was down he was surrounded by hundreds of excited villagers, who insisted on touching the aircraft. Some of the smaller boys experimented by putting pencils through its tail, much to the displeasure of the pilot.

Being aware of the euphoria, Ellison had asked the police to come for the landing of Air Commodore Fellowes in his Puss Moth. The Police were just able to hold the crowds back for the landing, before they surged around the aircraft. Clydesdale and McIntyre were surprised that their arrival was such a local sensation:

> We had not expected to create such a stir and had no desire to be impeded by public attention in the work ahead of us. We were never to get quite free of this embarrassing interest and the small as well as the big machines were ultimately removed to Lalbalu. Even that did not defeat the Indians. They were fascinated and suspicious by turns, but they could not overcome their curiosity, and it was impossible to convince them that we were ordinary human beings.[8]

They had received assistance wherever they had been across India, from Indians and British alike, and their arrival had brought them closer to Mount Everest, whose ice rocks and snows concealed the bones of many men who had failed to reach its summit.

6 UNDER THE HIMALAYAS

IT WAS AS well that the Police Department had been warned in advance as to the coming of the Westland aircraft. Public fascination in India was great and it was well known that the aircraft concerned would fly so high that the airmen inside would die, without the most modern scientific oxygen apparatus. They would also have to wear clothing heated all over so that they would not freeze. Rumours had begun to circulate of a fantastic kind, one being that the aviator would also try to fly around the moon especially as the moon would be visible in daytime at roughly the same time as the flight to Everest.

The members of the Expedition were astonished at the extent of the interest, and they were delighted with Etherton's news on his return from Nepal that he had secured the good wishes and blessing of the Maharajah. He had persuaded the Maharajah that their plan was sound, that the aircraft would be able to reach their objective with relatively little risk of crashing, and that the results would be of value to science and geography. Etherton was also pleased to learn that the Maharajah had made a speech after reviewing his Armed Forces. The gathering of Nepalese troops was greater than ever before. Nepal would act in the interests of Nepal, but as

The Darbhanga bungalow

and when emergencies occurred, like that in 1914 at the outset of the Great War, they could be trusted to do their best to support the just cause of the British Government, "their great friend and ally".[1]

In India as well everyone in authority gave assistance. The Maharajah of Darbhanga had even lent his bungalow to the Expedition. It consisted of large rooms next to a verandah, surrounding three of its sides, and about a mile away was the private race course of the Raja of Banaili, who lent the members of the Expedition a fleet of cars. He offered them fifteen and seemed astounded when one lorry and three cars were all that they required.

At Lalbalu, some ten miles away, three canvas hangars for the aircraft had been erected and several members of the R.A.F. party were present there all the time, near to the Westland aircraft. The base camp for the pilots and observers was at Purnea. It had at one time possessed a thriving indigo trade, but with stiff competition there had been a contraction of business. Jute and sugar cane were now common crops. It was there that the party became involved in a steady routine of hard work. All the different members of the Expedition came together for the first time,

The veranda of the Darbangha bungalow

equipping the camp and establishing friendly contact with the neighbours of the district.

With the pilots and members of the Expedition came Post Office telegraphists—so that Shepherd could send back his reports for *The Times* speedily—R.A.F. mechanics, Captain Bennett who was the Doctor, Came the engineer and Tom Smith and his wife, who moved in from their indigo plantation to make Expedition members comfortable. Clydesdale and McIntyre wrote that they "felt like an invasion and no doubt gave that impression to the kindly people who received us so well".[2]

The Bungalow of the Maharajah of Darbhanga accommodated Clydesdale and Blacker in one room, Air Commodore and Mrs. Fellowes in another, McIntyre and Shepherd of *The Times* in a third room, and Ellison and Captain Bennett, the Doctor, in a fourth room. A small room was also equipped as a darkroom for developing photographs. The luggage came from the station a mile and a half away on a cart pulled by bullocks.

They did not take long to settle that evening, and were watchful lest they mistakenly trod on a snake in the dark. Next morning and each morning thereafter they were up with the dawn at 5.15 a.m., so that an assessment could be made to see if weather conditions were suitable. The meteor-

Left to right: Clydesdale and Blacker talk to Mr Gupta, measuring the windspeed, through his theodolyte

ologist, Gupta, would arrive at about 6 a.m. with a detailed report, having supplied a forecast as to the likely weather the night before. If the early report had been favourable, Fellowes would carry out an early morning reconnaissance the next day to check conditions for an assault on Mount Everest. Breakfast would follow these discussions on wind conditions and Ellison, acting as transport officer, made certain that the R.A.F. contingent at Lalbalu received their breakfast early.

The airmen were sleeping in tents near the aerodrome, where there were risks that they might receive nocturnal visits from crocodiles and tigers, but a supply of rifles and ammunition made them feel secure. Of more importance were the storms which threatened to blow away their tents. Their food was brought from kitchens in Purnea by the fleet of cars, and as soon as the smaller aircraft were transferred to Lalbalu motor transport was essential if the pilots were to reach the main airfield quickly.

The local planters made the members of the Expedition honorary members of their Club, and after an evening's entertainment there the visitors would return to the bungalow across the golf course, torches lit to avoid snakes—a necessary precaution brought home to them by the discovery of a lethal cobra in the drawing room of the Darbhanga bungalow. Its life had been brought to an end by the swift intervention of an Indian helper.

Bathing shared with elephants

Tennis and golf were also available for recreation in off-duty hours and the Maharajah of Darbhanga had extended an open invitation to use the pool on a nearby estate. The pool had a double function of storing water to combat dry seasons and was situated near huts and farm buildings. Though the doctor considered the water dangerous to drink, they enjoyed watching the villagers bathe off the backs of submerged elephants. This pool, however, was some ten miles distant and McIntyre and the others welcomed the discovery of a smaller pool near the aerodrome at Lalbalu. As it was part of the Panar river, its bed was largely covered with weeds and creepers. Came, the engineer, employed some Indian fishermen to clear these and from then on the pool was used for bathing. A diving board was erected on poles of bamboo, with a ladder attached to it, and as the rubber beds for the aircraft had not been used, two of them were inflated and converted into floating rafts.

All of this was a pleasant enough diversion after hours of hard work on the aircraft, on the ground and in the air, and for long enough no danger was evident. Then, over a period of several days they noticed what they believed to be a piece of old wood drifting in the pool. Their suspicions seemed without foundation when they threw clods of earth at it to no avail and bathing continued, though at a distance from the piece of flotsam. One day, however, an airman found a crocodile, seven feet long, sunning itself on the bank shortly before lunch. Further bathing was obviously discouraged, and each morning for the next few days, an armed task force was dispatched to deal with the menace.

David McIntyre above the crocodile-infested pool

They would arrive before dawn, lie down on their raincoats in the dew-covered grass, and wait for the crocodile to present them with a target. Its presence was identified by the sighting of a dentist bird, a species associated with crocodiles, which would flutter across whenever the snub nose showed itself above the surface. The Expedition members had little time, though, to concentrate on this task along with their other duties, and for the first three mornings they could only see the nose of the reptile. They did see enough of it, however, to know that it was not a fish-eating alligator but a flesh-eating crocodile. The only place where a bullet was certain to kill it was behind where its ears might have been, if it had any, in the softer part of its shell in the spine. A bullet hitting anywhere else would leave a wounded and ferocious crocodile in their pool.

At last an opportunity presented itself one morning. McIntyre saw the crocodile with its neck underwater. He aimed at the spot where he thought the neck must be and as he fired Shepherd and Ellison blazed away as well. There was "a great swirl of discoloured water"[3] and the crocodile disappeared, diving to the bottom of the pool. Two days later its dead body was found floating on the water. The aircraftmen took the skin from its underside and within a short period vultures had eaten the rest of it, excluding the skeleton and outer shell.

After this incident bathing was resumed with caution, with two Indian fishermen being employed to look out for man-eating crocodiles from the tops of bamboo poles whose base pierced the bottom of the pond. Previously the members of the Expedition had associated elephants, snakes, tigers and crocodiles with Rudyard Kipling's stories of Mowgli. Now they were aware of the reality, especially so when another crocodile had to be shot some days later.

There were other forms of wild life roaming around. One night jackals appeared in a park, attempting to steal the bones of one of the guard dogs. But perhaps one of the most colourful episodes involving animals related to a baby elephant with its mother. McIntyre described what happened.

> As we sat discussing plans outside the bungalow we noticed an enormous elephant with a mahout perched between its ears, followed by a tiny baby elephant. We hailed the mahout and invited him to bring his caravan over for our closer inspection. The little chap was attractive with ridiculous little baby hairs all down his trunk and as playful as a kitten for all his ton of weight.
>
> We found that by pushing his face in he could be persuaded to afford wonderful sport by offering chase. After about half an hour's fun and games he began to lose his temper. . . .
>
> Our Chief Pilot, Clydesdale, appeared on the scene and in all innocence approached to pat it in the friendliest manner. Baby gave him one dirty look and shot at him like a rocket. My Commanding Officer disappeared round the corner of the bungalow at a modest 15 miles per hour followed by baby at a modest 14.9, but improving. . . .
>
> One obtained a splendid view of them rounding the first bend with the chief pilot fairly clear in front of the dust cloud; a little later there was only the cloud to be seen with the tail end of the elephant showing dimly through the haze. The race finished amid great excitement when the quarry blazed a new track through the grandstand. Baby seeing humans screaming off in every direction, became a trifle confused, hesitated, decided not to trust his weight on the bungalow floors and retired very ruffled from the race. Our conference could not be resumed until the chief pilot had returned, hot and dusty from a distant mango grove.[4]

All that happened in the background, whilst serious work was in progress for the rest of the day. Each large machine was watched over closely by its pilot and observer. Together, with the airmen and Cyril Pitt and Francis Burnard, they ensured that the material that they would have to use remained in good working order. In particular the wire rigging of the aircraft had to be checked, since the difference between the temperatures could be as great as twenty degrees. It proved to be invaluable that the two key experts from the Bristol Aeroplane Company and from the Westland Aircraft Company, Pitt and Burnard, were constantly present, looking for maladjustments, shrinkages and expansions. The valves, sparking plugs and airscrews had to be checked, and some evenings work continued until midnight under the lights in the hangars.

Members of the expedition preparing for the flight

Fuelling the Houston Westland, while awaiting the return of the reconnaissance machine

The days were long and hard, starting at 5.30 a.m. and continuing until 6 p.m. with special jobs being completed later. They had to examine every part of the aircraft, after every flight, however brief. Pitt and Burnard felt that the reputation of their companies was at stake, and all their energy and experience was devoted to protecting the aircraft and the lives of those who would fly in them.

In his spare time Pitt wrote an article for the British *Evening Post* giving his first impressions, describing the villages nearby as consisting mainly of mudhuts, naked children, lean cows, goats, monkeys in the trees and crocodiles beside the rivers, all very different from his native West Country.

Apart from anything else the heat was very great in comparison to the weather in Britain. The daylight heat could affect the large airscrews, unless they were kept in the shade. When they were in the sunlight the wood of the propellors seemed to shrink, so that the nuts and bolts securing them had to be tightened up often. Different parts of the aircraft had to be protected from clouds of dust blown by the wind. The oxygen apparatus was covered by cloth, and the camera had layers of wrappings. Even this was not enough, and the camera had to be dismantled after use, the parts being wrapped and packed in boxes in the bungalow under lock and key.

What happened every day depended upon the state of the weather. Here

Mr Gupta issuing his findings as to wind speeds

they received the most up to date scientific information available. Each night the pilots were given the forecast for the following day of the weather around Mount Everest. This information came from Calcutta by telegram from the Indian Meteorological Service and was supplemented by Gupta, the meteorological officer. He and his Indian assistants would send up hydrogen balloons for the purpose of determining the direction and strength of the wind at a variety of different heights. Gupta would watch them through his theodolite, until they were out of sight. He knew the rate at which the balloons ascended, and by calculating the angle of the drift, he could assess the speed of the winds, up to a height of 25,000 feet. The pilots considered that Gupta had an "almost uncanny weather sense",[5] and his evidence gave them virtually all that they required to know.

Air Commodore Fellowes would fly the Puss Moth at dawn to confirm in detail with his own eyes the weather conditions over the Himalayas. If the prospect of reasonable weather was likely, the pilots made their calculations as to wind direction and force, plotted their course, and estimated the speed of climb. The observers would put their cameras together in readiness for filming. All this might take ninety minutes.

Clydesdale experienced the feelings of frustration when time after time they could not fly:

> Often we stood to, ready to start the engines when the Air Commodore returned to the aerodrome, only to be told that though the wind strength was reasonable, there were heaps of piled cloud on the mountains; or that a clear dawn was changing into a cloudy morning as the sun warmed the drifting vapours over the plains and encouraged these currents to condense as they reached the ice-fields; or that a fine clear day was being ruined by high winds over the mountain tops, as might be gathered from the length of Everest's plume, streaming away sometimes six or seven miles to leeward. Sometimes this procedure was unnecessary for the hurricane winds, which came sweeping across the flat lands, told their own tale and kept us busy weighting down and repairing the tents.[6]

The winds would rage at sixty miles per hour and would rend the canvas roofs of the hangars. A great many sacks of sand were placed on the tents to weigh down their sides. The aircraft too had to be tied to the ground, and the canvas would be laced together immediately after the wind tore it. This work was carried out continually. The gales would also flood some of the tents of the aircraftmen but apart from the discomfort, they were reasonably well off with electrical lighting in their tents, so that they could dine and engage in reading each night.

When the weather was not excessively stormy, opportunities were available to Barkas, the film director, to proceed with his programme of recording the history of their mission. He insisted that wherever possible, when filming took place, it should be accompanied by sound recordings as well. The production team numbered seven, including two sound

Starting the engine

technicians with an assistant, three cameramen and the director himself. At the outset, when the aircraft were being constructed at Yeovil, it was discovered that in order to have all the required film equipment, the entire aircraft would have to be rebuilt around the camera.

Under the business management of Connochie the end result had been a compromise, with modifications enabling the cameramen to take film at all heights. The two cine camera operators, Bonnett and Fisher, had considerable experience in the air, and their previous rehearsal in a low temperature chamber meant that they knew how to ensure that the cameras worked well at temperatures of at least minus sixty degrees centigrade. Two other members of the film crew, Read and Sweeny, checked that the sound recording equipment would function effectively under a tropical sun. Various telephoto lenses had to be tested for different kinds of film, including infra-red film.

There was so much which had to be transported that it was taken by sea, and 80,000 feet of film were packed into thirty wooden cases. Trunks were filled with spare parts, batteries, and other materials. A huge crate was required for an electric generator and petrol motor to charge the batteries, when better facilities did not exist. The cameras, tripods, stands, microphones, cables, accumulators and amplifiers were all taken on board, the entire diverse paraphernalia being worth in the region of £10,000.

At Karachi the film crew had filmed the cranes lifting out the crates with the Westland aircraft inside, and the workshops at the aerodrome. On the way to Delhi in the Houston-Westland, Bonnett filmed areas of interest, and from there to Lalbalu Fisher took his place. The film across India revealed only a few items of great interest as the haze was hard to penetrate. At the aerodrome Barkas had requested the pilots to take off and land so that he could film. The pilots would put on their heated suits, with goggles and helmet, in spite of the sweltering heat of the Indian plains, and when he had shot enough film, this activity was stopped, for too much changing might adversely affect the electrical wires heating the suits.

He would also film the conferences held for planning future developments. At such meetings, Clydesdale and McIntyre might be discussing navigation problems, with Blacker interested in the prospects of filming and the Air Commodore watching over all proceedings. Doctor Bennett and Ellison would be discussing the question of getting food supplies to the airmen at the aerodrome and Shepherd would be drafting his despatches for *The Times*. Only Etherton might be elsewhere, obtaining assistance of one kind or another from the local residents.

Barkas was gathering every kind of information on film, with the intention of giving the facts a dramatic importance, building up to the climax of the actual flight over Everest, the great mountain telling the best and final part of his story. So virtually every detail was recorded day after day. He would film the markets with Indians looking astonished at the aircraft flying above them and the elephants with their passengers passing the aircraft and the villages. He would demand that a flight took place when the market was thronged with hundreds of people.

After analysing weather reports and ruling out the possibility of an attempt for the first flight over Everest, Clydesdale and McIntyre would oblige Barkas. They would be filmed taking off and landing, flying directly over the camera team, and climbing in and out of the aircraft.

The film crew had problems with the heat, which at its height caused the film to crumble and to stick, and there had to be a certain amount of readjustment. Sometimes the heat of the sun would enter the camera, melting the perforation holes of the film. When the heat was very great the filming might have to stop, and often one of the local villagers would be employed to shade the camera and film with a dark umbrella. By dint of relentless endurance, the necessary filming took place.

Slopes of the Kanchenjunga group through the wires of the aircraft

Film of the mountains on the way to Everest was taken by one of the aircraft up to the lower reaches of Mount Kanchenjunga, as this did not involve a flight over Nepal, where permission had been given for two

Map of the route from Lalbalu to Mount Everest

flights only. This was done by placing a film camera under one wing, so that the scene could be clearly identified without the rigging of the aircraft being in the way.

For filming purposes Barkas wanted the first flight over Mount Everest to be marked by the dropping of a smoke bomb, while Bonnett in McIntyre's aircraft would photograph it. Clydesdale opposed this suggestion as "an objectionable piece of theatricality to introduce into a serious task".[7] He did not wish to be distracted from concentrating upon his exact course and flying and he was not at all sure that there would be much smoke in thin air at the height of 35,000 feet. In any case he did not wish McIntyre to risk colliding with him by keeping too close. Clydesdale's opposition was not well received by the film crew. Even if the lives of the

A gathering of the members of the expedition, including the RAF mechanics and Shepherd of The Times

pilots might well be hanging in the balance when the first flight would be attempted, a considerable sum had been paid for the film rights, and it was felt that the pilots should do their best to accommodate the sensational schemes of Mr. Barkas.

But before any action could be taken on this proposal, on the evening of 2nd April, news from Mr. Gupta and the Calcutta Meteorological Office indicated that the weather the next morning would be good enough to make the assault on Mount Everest.

After dinner, Air Commodore Fellowes, the pilots and observers had a final conference. At that meeting the die was cast. The following morning, come what may, the two aircraft would set out to accomplish their mission. Purnea had brought them to a kind of "grim unity",[8] which would persist until the prime cause of it had been resolved one way or another. Their fourteen months of preparation and training were now at an end. Within a few hours they would have flown over Mount Everest or be dead.

Clydesdale found himself wondering if he had remembered everything he had to get ready, and then it came back to him that there was something important he had forgotten. Before leaving Hendon aerodrome his mother had given him a mascot, whose identity she had refused to reveal. He found it and unpacked it out of its wrapping of brown paper. Inside was a medallion of blue enamel, showing Saint Christopher, the patron Saint of all travellers in dangerous places, battling his way through torrents of water. He put it away in his flying suit. Wherever he would go the next day, the medallion of Saint Christopher would travel with him.

7 MOUNT EVEREST CONQUERED

BY DAWN ON 3 April the pilots and observers were rushing around the Darbhanga Bungalow. Air Commodore Fellowes departed, after a shortened breakfast, to fly the Puss Moth on a reconnaissance mission so that he would have his assessment ready by the time that the two Westland aircraft were ready to go.

At first light Gupta had released a balloon, but the dust haze obscured it from sight. He was at work, about to release a second balloon when the pilot and observers passed him on the way to Lalbalu. He was at the centre of a group of his Indian assistants staring through his theodolite as the balloon ascended, shouting out the detailed readings for his assistants to record. It was going to take some ninety minutes for the hydrogen balloon to reach 35,000 feet, so transport had been arranged for him to follow on to Lalbalu with his information.

The advance party bounced along the road, each man holding a camera or part of the equipment, to protect it from the jolts of the drive. The cameras were so delicate that each night every item had to be cleaned and wrapped up in two layers of newspaper. Installing them in the two aircraft would take nearly half an hour.

At the aerodrome the R.A.F. ground crew were working on the large aircraft. The canvas hangars were opened, and the aircraft were pushed on to the landing strip. The cameras were fitted; the oxygen cylinders were installed and connected, and the engines, airframes and rigging were tested. The pilots and observers climbed into their suits, ensuring that their straps, oxygen pipes and heating cables were in the correct position. The navigation was checked again depending upon the different and increasing wind speeds at greater heights. For an hour they waited in suspense and excitement for their journey into the unknown.

At the same time as they saw the Air Commodore in his Puss Moth, descending through the haze towards the aerodrome, the car driving Gupta speeded past the Indian guards at the entrance to Lalbalu with his estimates as to the force of the winds at high altitudes. Under the wing of the Puss Moth the facts were revealed.

Gupta, Clydesdale and Blacker

The wind levels were 67 mph at 28,000 feet and 58 mph at 30,000 feet. Earlier on it had been laid down that there should be no attempt to fly over Everest if the winds were above 40 mph. The reason for this was that a wind from the West would make the aircraft drift sideways off course. To counteract this they would have to steer into the wind on a fixed course, taking into account the drift. Steering into wind would have the same result as flying much further without wind, and the stronger the wind the more fuel would be consumed. But the flight was not automatically ruled out by Gupta's information, since this was the first time that they had found the wind to be below 100 mph. After making some calculations, McIntyre announced that if the aircraft were able to stay some fifteen minutes in the vicinity of Everest, in the face of a 67 mph wind from the West, they could just have enough fuel to return. If they waited for better conditions, they might have to wait a long time, and such an opportunity might not come again, with the monsoon about to arrive.

The Air Commodore's news had been slightly more encouraging than that of Gupta. He had taken the Puss Moth up to 17,000 feet, where he had developed engine trouble, and while he had only been able to see the mountains dimly, the haze being in evidence, no clouds were visible. The weather conditions were not ideal, but they were a marked improvement on those of previous days. After careful consideration the Air Commodore authorised the flight with the word "Go".[1]

They made haste but with care, as the more they perspired the colder they would be over Everest. After checking their heavy wind, water and fireproof flying suits, lined with electrical heating, they pulled on their boots heated along the soles and up the legs, and joined to the suit by electrical gear at the knees. The helmet had even more wires running in and out of it. Telephones were attached to the ears and the eyes were surrounded by the electrically heated goggles and the large mask with its

Etherton hands to Bonnet in the Wallace the Everest mail, including a letter to King George V

oxygen feed pipe and microphone. This had to fit closely to the face over the mouth, nose and chin, and left little room for comfort. Numerous cables from the telephone, microphone and goggles were incorporated into the flying suit, connected to the back of the helmet, the oxygen feedpipe passing over the right shoulder of the pilot and under his arm to the dashboard, the other leads from the various items of clothing being attached to sockets beside the pilot.

The cameras were loaded and the giant Pegasus engines were started, their fuel tanks full. Barkas, the film director, was in his element, filming the Air Commodore and Etherton shaking hands with the film participants before they clambered into the machines. A dramatic and optimistic touch was introduced by handing up to Bonnett in the Wallace the Everest mail, consisting of letters intimating the Expedition's success to King George V, the Prince of Wales and Lady Houston. Barkas, anxious to miss nothing, wished the pilots to take off in the best possible position for his filming. He wrote later:

> I well remember the moment of departure, the pilots giving the signals for the chocks to be removed, the engines warming up, the shimmering heat-haze making the air quiver as we looked cross the aerodrome, the blast of hot air in

The mechanics and RAF ground crew wish them good luck

the slipstream of the propellors, and the last view of Bonnett in one machine and Blacker in the other, goggled and masked, as they closed down the covers of the cockpit for the early part of the climb. Then . . . the wait, the mental calculations as to how many flying hours the machines could manage before we need feel any anxiety for their return, the frequent glances at wrist watches when the time came to expect the first distant sound of their return and the listening look in people's eyes as they talked of other things.[2]

Behind Clydesdale sat Blacker, and McIntyre, flying a short distance in the rear, had as his observer Bonnett. Both aircraft rose steadily on a course of 342 degrees, and it was confirmed that all apparatus was functioning properly. Blacker and Bonnett had some forty-six jobs to perform, none of which could be forgotten without risking the failure of the camera survey.

With much activity in the cockpits the two aeroplanes climbed into the dust haze, seeing the river Panar with its dried up bed and its two-mile wide stretch of grass. After thirty minutes the reached Forbesganj and swung to the left, crossing the border of Nepal, East of Gograha. At 10,000 feet, by a prearranged agreement, McIntyre came close to Clydesdale's aircraft, signalled to him "All Correct" and received the same response in return. However, McIntyre was slightly concerned about his survey cameras and their control, and Clydesdale found that the intercom between himself and Blacker started buzzing as soon as it was tested. The buzzing would not stop and became annoying since neither of them could hear a word spoken by the other. They had to communicate by passing handwritten notes to each other.

As they climbed further to 16,000 feet the plains below became invisible, and they could only glimpse the foothills in the vicinity of the gorge of the Kosi River. The pilots had hoped to begin their survey above Komaltar, but it was not possible to see through the dust haze, and they had to guess as to its position, hoping that the survey cameras would do their job well. All that they could see were glimpses of forests on the mountains of Nepal with the Arun river in its deep valley.

Cydesdale opened up his engines to full power and at 19,000 feet both aircraft surfaced from the haze to witness an astounding sight some fifty miles away:

> We found ourselves emerging into the most vividly clear atmosphere with unlimited visibility. The aeroplanes seemed to be enclosed within a semi-circle of the most gigantic mountains in the world. This time they really looked enormous, because we were seeing them from much closer range than we had ever seen them before. Just to the right of the aeroplane's nose as it rose clear of the murk, the summit of Mount Everest appeared with its plume, like the smoke of a volcano, stretching out to the East.
> A little further to the right stood the majestic Makalu which, because of the angle of our approach, looked even higher than Everest although in fact about

The panorama in its startling white beauty, Everest to the left in cloud and Makalu to the right

1,200 feet lower. Something like 100 miles to the East rose the great massif of Kanchenjunga not appreciably nearer to us than it had already been on Sunday reconnaissance flights. Yet seeming to be much nearer on account of the extraordinarily clear air and the greater height from which we were seeing it. To the left was the remarkable pointed peak of Gauri Sankar, about 100 miles West of Everest.

This panorama presented itself to us in its startling white beauty, glistening in the bright morning sunshine and making a magnificent spectacle. The dust haze, completely obscuring the foothills, rose well above the snow line, with the result that this arc of great mountains appeared detached from the earth, and suggested an eerie land floating in a drab sea somewhere between earth and sky.[3]

As they rose higher more peaks appeared side by side, until countless mountains in the Himalayas appeared in all their vastness.

Clydesdale was finding difficulty with his oxygen. He had turned it on whilst on the ground, and he had economised with the supply of oxygen, to be certain that there was plenty in reserve in case the flight over the summit took longer than anticipated. Blacker passed a note to Clydesdale requesting more oxygen, and at the same time Clydesdale felt his eyesight begin to fail. Suddenly he had a violent attack of cramp in both feet. He turned on the emergency and the main supply of oxygen: after a number of deep breaths the cramp disappeared and he could see normally again. He then turned off the emergency supply but kept the main supply on at full strength. The tests completed at Farnborough had given him the knowledge of how to deal with just such a situation.

Mount Everest with its snow plume streaking to the right towards Mount Makalu

By this time the pilots had planned to be at the height of 33,000 feet. They had, though, flown lower than intended in an attempt to locate Komaltar, the proposed starting point of their survey work. Now more height would have to be obtained urgently in order to clear the summit of Mount Everest.

The Houston-Westland climbed up to a height of 31,000 feet, and Clydesdale began to feel more relaxed. Then, only a few minutes from the summit, he encountered the most unpleasant reality of his life. He and McIntyre had prepared for every conceivable eventuality. They knew that in the lee of mountains there could be downdraughts, while on the other side the wind would be deflected upwards, with up currents near the summit. They had plotted this course with the aim of avoiding any possible downdraughts. However, there had been a strong wind from the West, and to their horror the truth dawned that they were approaching Mount Everest on the leeward side, having been blown off course: "Almost as soon as the thought occurred to me, we encountered a powerful and persistent down draught due to the deflection of the wind over Mount Everest. . . . It was disturbing to find ourselves in a downward current whose velocity and extent could not be foretold."[4] Immediately his aircraft was sucked down towards the mountains.

The Houston Westland about to be sucked down in a downdraught in the direction of the north east ridge of Mount Everest

Blacker, who was working hard with the cameras, recalled vividly what happened:

The scene was superb and beyond description. The visibility was extraordinary and permitted the whole range to be seen on the western horizon. The size of the mountains stunned the senses, the stupendous scale of the scenery and the clear air confounded all estimates of size and distance.

So I went on, now exposing plates, now lifting the heavy cine-camera, to run off 50 feet or so of film. I crouched down, struggling to open the hatchway, to take a photograph through the floor. Everything by now, all the metal parts of the machine, was chilled with the cold. The fastenings were stiff and the metal slides had almost seized. I struggled with them, and I squeezed my mask on to my face to get all the oxygen possible. I had to pause and suddenly, with the door half-open I became aware, almost perceptibly, of a sensation of dropping through space.

The floor of the machine was falling away below us. I grasped a fuselage strut and peered through my goggles at the altimeter needle. It crept, almost swung, visibly as I looked at it in astonishment, down through a couple of thousand feet. In this great downdraught of the winds, it seemed as though we should never clear the crags of the South Peak on the way to Everest now towering above us.[5]

McIntyre in the second aircraft was if anything in an even worse position. The Wallace had been climbing more slowly than the Westland-Houston, owing to the extra weight of Bonnett's heavy cameras and film, and he was flying behind and below. McIntyre noticed that the wind was much more powerful than anticipated, and he estimated that the wind plume from Everest was streaking down the twelve-mile range to Makalu with the force of a hurricane. Although the Wallace's engine was operating at full strength, he was being blown down on to the Western side of Makalu. A short time before his aircraft had been higher than the summit. Now he was at least 1000 feet below the jagged mountain looking down on him.

> We were in a tremendous down-rush of air. Though the machine continued to climb, it was climbing in an air current that was carrying it down at much greater velocity. Two thousand feet were lost before the down-rush cushioned itself out on the glacier beds.
> We were in a serious position. The great bulk of Everest was towering above us to the left, Makalu down-wind to the right and the connecting range dead ahead, with a hurricane wind doing its best to carry us over and dash us on the knife-edge side of Makalu.
> I had the feeling that we were hemmed in on all sides, and that we dare not turn away to gain height afresh. There was plenty of air-space behind us, yet it was impossible to turn back. A turn to the left meant going back into the down-current and the peaks below; a down-turn round to the right would have taken us almost instantly into Makalu at 200 miles per hour.
> There was nothing we could do but climb straight ahead and hope to clear the lowest point in the barrier range. . . . With the aircraft heading almost straight into the wind, we crabbed sideways towards the ridge, unable to determine if we were level with it or below.[6]

It seemed to him that he might well be swept into the North East Ridge of Everest even at its lowest point. Clydesdale at this time was ahead and to the left. Each pilot had agreed earlier that in the event of an emergency, each should act independently, and the down draught had in any case carried McIntyre's aircraft even further below than the Westland-Houston.

Clydesdale felt his aircraft being clawed downwards in the air current, although his Pegasus engine was pulling at full power and the aircraft was climbing as steeply as possible at its highest flying angle. He no longer flew by instruments but relied entirely on sight, watching Lhotse, the Southern peak. Blacker had the hatchway below him and could see the rock buttresses of the Southern ridge coming closer and closer. Suddenly they passed over the Southern Peak by a few feet. Clydesdale would never say just how close he came to colliding with the mountain, other than to admit that the peak had been cleared by a more minute margin than he cared to think about then or ever.

McIntyre's problems were every bit as great. He could see that if he was to clear the East Ridge, it would only be by the narrowest of margins:

> A fortunate up-current just short of the ridge carried us up by a few feet and we scraped over. The North East ridge appeared to sweep us vertically from our port wing-tips to the summit, and we could see straight down the sheer North side to the glacier cradles at the base of Everest . . .

At this stage he had to circle three times, turning to the left in order to gain sufficient height to make the attempt to fly over the summit of Everest.

> We had to turn very carefully towards Everest and then back over the ridge again with the little height we had gained and face the same flight over again. This business of turning towards the end of a down-draught in order to climb seems even in retrospect a mad risk. The mind was obsessed by the knowledge that we must avoid being blown back on Makalu and yet must approach dangerously close to it in order to have sufficient space for a slow, gentle turn to the right without being caught in the down-rush. The invisible menace of the down-draught had all the qualities of a nightmare. One had to try and imagine its limits and position from the topography. . . .
> An abnormal effort was required to make the decision and risk that turn towards the unseen down-rush, and then crab over the ridge once more. Three times we had to repeat this performance, gaining a little height to venture round the North side and over the top of Everest.[7]

To complicate matters further, Bonnett had trouble with his oxygen. He was hard at work with the cameras, seemingly oblivious to the immense danger he was in each time the Wallace just cleared the ridge. As the aircraft flew towards the North side of Mount Everest, Bonnett was filling his camera with film and trod on his oxygen feed pipe, fracturing it. Feeling weakness come over him, he subsided on to the floor, and with admirable coolness found the broken feed pipe, binding his handkerchief around the fracture. He attempted to rise with his heavy camera and photograph again but was overcome through lack of oxygen and fell down unconsious.

McIntyre saw Bonnett slip down and, disturbed at what had happened to him, resolved to fly over the summit of Mount Everest photographing with the survey camera, and then to lose height so that Bonnett, if he was still alive, would have a good chance of recovering. As these thoughts passed through his mind, for the first time since entering the down-draught he caught sight of Clydesdale's aircraft above and ahead of him, flying straight for the summit.

After just scraping over Lhotse, Clydesdale flew through part of Everest's plume and experienced a considerable air bump, throwing the aircraft suddenly into an upward drift on the windward side of the mountain. The

Looking down on the summit of Everest for the first time, 3 April 1933

aircraft gained height quickly and with the Pegasus engine at maximum power it surged over the top of Mount Everest, clearing the summit at 10.05 a.m.. Clydesdale would later say that after experiencing the awfulness of being swept down in the downdraught, and only just escaping collision, entering the updraught was like being swept up into heaven.

Blacker watched as the aeroplane "came to the curved chisel like Summit of Everest, crossing it, so it seemed to me, just a hair's breadth over its menacing summit. The crest came up to meet me as I crouched peering through the floor, and I almost wondered whether the tail skid would strike the summit."[8] In fact the aircraft cleared the summit by about 500 feet, having cleared the earlier hurdle which so nearly killed them. Clydesdale's thoughts were now on those who had come so near to conquering Everest on an earlier occasion.

I had always cherished the faint hope that it might be possible visually or by photograph, to establish that Mallory and Irvine, who lost their lives so gloriously in 1924, and were last seen attacking the final 1000 feet of Everest had actually reached the summit. I had always liked to think that they had

Looking steeply down on the actual summit of Everest with Makalu beyond

The Western end of the Chamlang range taken from almost over Everest

conquered the mountain after the gallant effort which deprived them of their lives.

As I came over the top, I tilted the right wing and looked down on the summit. It was just a passing glimpse, and it was not possible to discern any hint of human remains or of the apparatus of mountaineering.

I began to realise that it was most unlikely that any trace of them could be seen from the air. The East and South was the steep snow-face on which they could not have lain had they fallen, unless they had dropped into the small concave area just below the actual peak, and there they would almost undoubtedly have been covered with snow. Had they been lying on the black rock of the Northern face, broken and seamed and patched with snow-pockets, it would have been impossible to distinguish them, and it was highly improbable they had ventured beyond the summit to the precipitous fall on the Western side.[9]

Clydesdale noticed that the vertical camera was refusing to work, and he decided to give Blacker ever opportunity to obtain other photographs. He had previously arranged with McIntyre that after reaching the summit flying on a North-Westerly course, he would turn into the wind on the West of Mount Everest to photograph the unknown side of the great mountain.

Blacker at these moments had his head and shoulders in the slipstream photographing over the tail, so anxious was he to see every possible view. He was pleasantly surprised that the wind force was not great, and then he remembered that at sea level with much denser air, the wind would blow with greater force at the same true air speed.

We swooped over the summit and a savage period of toil began. The pilot swung the machine skilfully again towards the westward into the huge wind force sweeping downwards over the crest; so great was its strength that, as the machine battled with it and struggled to climb upwards against the downfall, we seemed scarcely to make headway in spite of our 120 miles per hour air speed. I crammed plate-holder after plate-holder into the camera, releasing the shutter as fast as I could, to line it on one wonderful scene after another. We were now for a few moments in the very plume itself, and as we swung round fragments of ice rattled violently into the cockpit.[10]

Clydesdale too had felt that the aircraft had seemed to be stationary, and had seen that the wind velocity appeared to be as great as the speed of the aircraft. He decided that the risk of continuing to fly relatively low above Mount Everest was too great in case the aircraft was suddenly sucked down in a down-draught on the mountainside. His first impressions that Everest was not unlike some of the peaks in the Alps, over which he had flown in Switzerland, changed rapidly when he saw the glacier on the East and Northern flanks of the North East ridge, and realised he was seeing more than he had bargained for "even on this mountain of mystery".[11] These contradictory thoughts crowded in on him, one after the other. The

The knife edge of Mount Makalu

proportions of Mount Everest were far greater than anything he had ever witnessed.

It was while Clydesdale was flying over Mount Everest for the second time that McIntyre had caught sight of him. McIntyre was climbing vigorously, having lost much more height, and the two aircraft passed each other to the North East of the summit. Blacker was photographing the North East Ridge making the best use of the time available. He took an oblique photograph of Everest over the tail, and then changed the film. By the time Blacker emerged again the aircraft had turned 180 degrees and was once more circling towards Everest while McIntyre went over the summit. Blacker who had been changing films while the aircraft was wheeling in the sky proceeded to train his camera on to Makalu, called "the Armchair of the Gods" by the Nepalese, thinking it was Everest, but Clydesdale touched him on the shoulder, indicating which was which, chuckling as he did so.

Blacker's oxygen pressure gauge showed signs of moving downwards, so he and Clydesdale knew that they only had a very short time to go in the vicinity of Everest. Clydesdale turned right, flying over the Rongbuk Glacier, and moved slowly down the valley halfway between the two peaks of Everest and Makalu, rejoining McIntyre in the process. They had only been in the neighbourhood of the summit for fifteen minutes. To Blacker it had seemed "like a lifetime from its amazing experiences and yet was all too short".

McIntyre on flying over the summit of Everest had thought that there was standing room for some four persons there and lamented the fact that with Bonnett unconscious the survey camera had not been working. Whilst turning to look at Bonnett, McIntyre with great suddenness experienced freezing cold around his nose and mouth. He had swivelled his head so far to look that the oxygen feed in his mask had fallen off and lay on his knee. With great speed he put it back in place, and had to hold it there continually. It was as well he acted very quickly for the consequences otherwise would almost certainly have been fatal.

With only one hand at the controls McIntyre lost height as quickly as was safe, in the hope that Bonnett might not be dead. It was when he reached the height of 8,000 feet over Forbesganj that his attention was attracted: "To my intense relief, Bonnett was struggling up from the floor tearing off mask and headgear. He was a nasty dark green shade but obviously alive and that was enough for the moment."

Some twenty minutes later at 11.25 a.m., three hours after take-off, they appeared over Lalbalu in perfect formation, and completed a perfect landing, their great flight at an end. McIntyre had a heat blister on one of his hands where there had been overheating in the electrical wires of a glove, and Bonnett, clutching the broken oxygen pipe, was looked at by Dr Bennett.

They hardly knew how lucky they were to be alive. Only the most meticulous technical preparations of both crews made them react with sufficient speed when threatened with a desperate lack of oxygen. A few more seconds and unconsciousness would have overwhelmed them, as had happened to Bonnett. His life had been saved by his coolness in tying a handkerchief around the fracture in the oxygen pipe. Similarly the

Returning from the successful aerial conquest of Mount Everest

immediate reaction of the pilots had been vital. If they had lost consciousness their aircraft might have disappeared virtually without trace into the uninhabited depths of the Himalayas.

As it was, the invisible and immense power of the down-draught on Everest's leeward side had brought them to the very edge of disaster. Each of the two aircraft only cleared the North East Ridge of Mount Everest by a few feet, narrowly avoiding crashing into the mountain. It brought home to them that the difference between triumph and tragedy is constituted by a thin dividing line, and they had only just managed to come down on the right side of it.

On landing they said nothing about the tremendous trials they had experienced at 30,000 feet. They wrenched off their clothing, so infuriatingly hot on the ground, and left the cameras and aircraft with the mechanics at Lalbalu. Their report could be written later. Overjoyed to be back they made for the swimming pool. There the threat of flesh-eating crocodiles seemed as nothing in comparison to the stupendous challenge of flying over the world's highest mountain, even in two of the most advanced aircraft ever to have been invented. As they dived into the pool, their experiences of Mount Everest fresh in their minds, they looked like men who felt that good fortune had smiled upon them.

8 TRIUMPH AND TRAGEDY

THE DOCTOR, CAPTAIN Bennett had carefully examined all four participants. Bonnett was shaken but had sustained no serious harm, and Blacker was tired, having made great exertions standing up in his open cockpit photographing Everest. The two pilots showed no signs of strain.

Whilst they were swimming, the letters which had been carried over Everest, addressed to the King, the Prince of Wales, Lady Houston and the Editor of *The Times* were posted. Thereafter the pilots and observers settled down to write their reports. Clydesdale's account outlined the main facts, accompanied by understatement. He even compared the flight to "an ordinary service flight at home".[1] In a sense he was correct, just as in the R.A.F. some years later pilots would carry out remarkable flights in action against the Third Reich, only to make light of them to others. But this was peacetime and the world press were not to be put off so easily. Blacker's report in particular appealed to the media.

It seemed to them as if one of the characters in Jules Verne's book *A Voyage to the Moon* had suddenly sprung to life, catching the spirit of the thrilling sights seen by the enthusiastic French scientist, and never before looked upon.[2] Indeed what the four men had witnessed of Mount Everest had never before been seen by man and their flight was the most spectacular one until, some thirty-six years later, men would attempt to travel by rocket to the moon. Blacker's account ended with the words:

> Our minds were numbed by that stark vision of beauty. Days must pass before we can appreciate what we have seen in those few sublime crowded minutes looking down on the world's last penetralia. Overriding the winds man's act has torn the veil from another of Nature's secrets. The uttermost peak is no longer inviolate.[3]

The information sent by Shepherd resulted in one of the longest reports ever published by *The Times,* which stressed the fact that the many months of preparation had resulted in a magnificent achievement.

Shepherd's original plan had been to say nothing about the failure of the survey cameras, but news had leaked to the world press from a journalist accompanying the film team. Shepherd had no alternative other than to tell the whole story. He mentioned that the only unfulfilled aspect was the fact that low visibility for a part of the flight and failure of the survey cameras to produce a complete mosaic of the country flown over, might necessitate a second flight. But what excited *The Times* was that this was the first time in the history of mankind that men had ever flown over the highest point on the earth's surface:

> Not even the camera will tell the whole of what the airmen, first of their kind in this have seen, nor can they perhaps ever hope to communicate it. It is almost like exploring the rainbow . . . to have proved its solidity of ice, snow and rock; to have looked down its many shaded slopes and folds, its glaciers and its desperate precipices; to have seen from above the irridiscence [sic] of its gigantic ice barriers; and to have gazed as it were over "the flaming walls of the world".[4]

At Purnea the telegrams began to flood in to Air Commodore Fellowes. He received one from Sir Clive Wigram: "The King offers you all his best congratulations on your great success."[5] The Prime Minister, Ramsay Macdonald, sent the message to Clydesdale, "My most hearty congratulations to you and your colleagues on your glorious achievement".[6] The Cabinet Ministers with a direct interest sent telegrams as well. The Secretary of State for India, Sir Samuel Hoare, sent a telegram to the Air Commodore: "Please accept and convey to all concerned my warmest congratulations on your splendid success in your Everest flight."[7] The Secretary of State for Air, Lord Londonderry, telegraphed: "Hearty congratulations to Clydesdale, McIntyre, Blacker and Bonnett on achieving first flight over Everest, and to all whose thorough and careful preparation made success possible."[8] The Air Commodore received a telegram from the Royal Aeronautical Society telling him, "The result is a high tribute to British machines, engines and pilots, and most thorough preparation which was bound to lead to ultimate success."[9] Fellowes responded to these telegrams by sending messages to the British companies who had given assistance, the Bristol Aeroplane Company receiving the telegram, "Sincerest thanks from all for splendid engines".[10]

Back in Britain Lady Houston had not been forgotten. She received the tribute from the Royal Aeronautical Society: "To you Great Britain owes the permanent possession of the Schneider Trophy, and now the undying prestige of this country being the first to conquer the highest point on the earth's surface".[11] In London the Mount Everest Flight Committee, which consisted of the same people as those who supported Britain winning the Schneider Trophy, including Lord Semphill and Wing Commander Orlebar, sent a further telegram to Lady Houston:

> The Committee of the Houston Mount Everest Flight send you their heartiest congratulations and warmest thanks for having once again been responsible for putting Britain in the forefront of world aviation. We feel that this magnificent achievement, only made possible by your generosity and patriotism, will advance Britain a great deal farther in the transport of the future.[12]

Lady Houston in turn sent a telegram to Clydesdale:

> Delighted to hear the glad news of your great victory over Everest. Send you my warmest congratulations and appreciation of your great achievement and of the pluck and courage you have shown. God bless you. Lucy Houston.[13]

Clydesdale received as well congratulations from Glasgow, the Lord Provost's message reading:

> On behalf of the citizens of Glasgow, I cordially congratulate you and your intrepid colleagues on the conquest of Mount Everest from the air. We are proud that a Glasgow man, and the head of the City of Glasgow Auxiliary Air Force, should have accomplished this historic achievement.[14]

McIntyre too received a telegram sending him heartiest congratulations. All these were indicative of a mood of elation, as well as relief, in Britain. The parents of Clydesdale and McIntyre were delighted and confessed to having been very anxious since anything might have happened and little in the way of help could be expected.[15]

This was only the beginning of the eruption in public interest. Lord Wakefield, a prominent industrialist, gave an interview to the press:

> The first flight over the world's highest mountain is an event in the history of aviation comparable almost to the first aerial crossings of the Channel and the Atlantic—equally hazardous and seemingly equally impossible. I rejoice with Lady Houston at this latest feat of British pilots, which ranks with our three records for maximum speed, altitude and distance.[16]

The events which had taken place gave a further edge to the lead of British aviation in the world. As it was, Flight Lieutenant Stainforth held the speed record, having flown at 407.5 mph Flight Lieutenant Uwins had won the height record by ascending to 43,976 feet, and Squadron Leader Gayford and Flight Lieutenant Nicholetts obtained the long distance record by flying 5,341 miles.[17] Much of the world press, like the *Hindu* in Madras, India, regarded the Everest Flight as "a record which is of the greatest world importance".[18] *The Times of India* called the Everest Flight "as important a landmark as any in the short history of aviation"[19] and the *Ceylon Observer* stated that it was an event "as notable as the first aerial crossing of the Atlantic".[20]

These sentiments were echoed in Europe. The *Central European Times* wrote:

> The British Flight over Mount Everest is a feat which will stand by itself in the History of Aviation. In point of careful and scientific preparation it is comparable to Rear Admiral Byrd's flight over the South Pole. In point of daring and navigation skills it is only equalled by Lindbergh's crossing of the Atlantic ocean.
>
> The battle against winds of a force of which plain-talking mortals have no conception, against treacherous up and down currents, against cold and lack of oxygen . . . is one which can only tempt men for whom the difficulty of the obstacles is but a call for further effort to overcome it.[21]

It was appreciated that the area of the Himalayas over which Everest towered was without question the most rugged highland area to be found in the world. The vast precipices, huge glaciers, deep crevasses and treacherous ridges are not excelled in their scope anywhere. For that reason those who lived nearest referred to the mountain range as the "Roof of the World," and some of them regarded Everest as the "Home of the Gods".

The assertion of man's mastery of the air by flying over the mighty crest for the first time made a strong appeal to the imagination, since Everest for centuries had appeared to symbolise the physically impossible. As the *West Middlesex Gazette* wrote "Such is the unconquerable spirit of man, nothing daunts him in his fight against the elements. . . . The news of the epic flight across the wind-swept summit of the highest mountain in the world comes as a tonic to peoples facing problems, that sometimes seem as insoluble as the top of Everest once seemed unattainable".[22] The fact that Mount Everest's secrets had been wrested from her, and that her summit had been filmed in the process meant that the most remarkable mountain in the world would soon be seen by countless people, and cease to be "No Man's Land".

"All the world", as the *Leicester Mail* put it, "will join in recognising the epic qualities of the flight, and Britain's prestige as the land of record makers and of intrepid explorers will be greatly enhanced".[23] The *East Anglian Daily Times* took up a theme along the same lines, that "The pioneering spirit which drove Shackleton and Scott to seek the polar wastes and hundreds of others to engage in enterprises of great pith and moment, no less daring, is still potent."[24]

In fact the Everest flight differed from both Lindbergh's flight across the Atlantic and Scott's expedition to reach the South Pole in 1912. Lindbergh's flight had been a substantial advance in the history of aviation, and Scott's Expedition had been primarily one of exploration. The Everest flight too was a pioneering flight, but there were elements in it of both exploration and aviation. Scott had not been the first man to reach the South Pole, the Norwegian, Amundsen, having arrived there first, but his had been an amazing example of endurance and courage. On their journey back lack of food, blizzards and sickness delayed them. Captain Oates, too ill to travel, in an act of selfless heroism had walked out into the snow storm, hoping that his sacrifice would save his friends. The remainder of the party and Scott had died only eleven miles from their depot.

Neither Lindbergh's flight, nor the Everest flight, could compare with the appalling weather conditions faced by Scott over a sustained period. In Lindbergh's case he had not been the first to fly the Atlantic. On 13th June, 1919 the British aviators, Alcock and Brown, had flown from Newfoundland to Ireland. But Lindbergh was the first man to fly solo, from Roosevelt Airfield, New York, to Le Bourget in France, a twenty-six hour flight, much of it at very low altitude and requiring great fortitude. It attracted more interest than the flight of Alcock and Brown, as it brought home to Europeans and North Americans that transatlantic air travel on a commercial basis would follow, as was the case within twelve years.

The Everest fliers, like Lindbergh, had not experienced extreme physical misfortune, but in the words of *The Times* they had to show "cool and skilful control of all the complexities of high altitude flying".[25] Their success represented a landmark in aviation. Just as Lindbergh had established that transatlantic air travel could take place, the Everest aviators had confirmed that no mountain need be a barrier to the passage of aircraft, and that there was no part of the world over which aircraft could not fly.

It had not just been a question of completing a daring and spectacular flight, but doing it, as the *Montreal Daily Star* put it, over "about the only notable part of the world left unvanquished by men".[26] It was hoped that the photographs taken could be of value to the mountaineers, who were approaching Everest from the Tibetan side, under Hugh Ruttledge. The final conquest would only take place when her summit had been reached by the foot of man.

The aviators had reminded many of the courage of the mountaineers and the *Manchester Evening Chronicle* wrote of them:

In this hour of triumph let us not forget the 13 who tried and died—men like Mallory and Irvine, who set forth never to return. The aerial feat is a memorial to the courage and death defying spirit of these pioneers of Everest. Let us honour both today's victors and the heroes of yesterday.[27]

The first flight over Mount Everest constituted a decisive leap forward in aviation development and technology, even if this triumph would only be one of many continuing developments. Before long commercial and civil airlines would be able to have linked air services around the world and it would be possible to fly from Britain to India within two days. The speed of communications would increase out of all proportion, and even Jules Verne's dream of men being propelled from the earth to the moon would become a reality.

What they had done would prompt the *Nottingham Journal* to declare that "Man is greater than all the earth he can stand upon".[28] Certainly the aircraft companies concerned, the Westland Aircraft Company at Yeovil and the Bristol Aeroplane Company at Bristol, which had supplied the aircraft frames and the engines respectively were delighted with this advertisement. The flight had demonstrated the reliability and excellence of their manufacture and of the other equipment, and was a credit to the skilled craftsmen who had worked on the machines.

More than any other person the success of the flight was due to Lady Houston, who provided the finance. The press in Christchurch, New Zealand, pointed out that if she had not given support, other aeroplanes might have been adapted in foreign countries, and the British air industry might have been pre-empted by its rivals. It was disconcerting to some to think that for the second time—the first being in relation to winning the Schneider Trophy—the British aviation industry had to rely on the bounty of an extremely wealthy, patriotic woman.[29]

As for Lady Houston herself, she gave an account as to the reasons for her financial support. She said:

The Expedition is like a fairy story from the *Arabian Nights*. Last summer, Lord Clydesdale called upon me and told me the flight over Everest would be the greatest thing aviation had ever attempted, and asked if I was inclined to interest myself in it.

After a long talk, I told him I did not want to help him commit suicide. This he laughingly declared was not a possibility, and he tried to persuade me that such an attempt would be as safe as a walk around Hampstead Heath on a foggy night.

My vivid imagination was thrilled by the romance of the idea, and my love of adventure eventually overcame all my scruples, and I agreed to help this deed of daring. . . .

I advised him first of all to see the great Orlebar, who trained two winners of the Schneider Trophy contest and "ask him" said I, to put you through all the most unpleasant stunts he can think of, as you must be absolutely fit before you start this most dangerous adventure.

This conquest of Everest is a splendid achievement, of which we Britishers and the people of India can be justly proud. I should like to see the Union Jack with "Everest" written across it, flying from every window here and in India.[30]

While she and the world press were rejoicing at the news from Purnea, they learnt about a tragedy which had taken place on the same day as the Everest flight. In the United States of America, the largest airship in the world, the *Akron*, built at a cost of more than £1 million, had crashed into the sea, causing 73 deaths. It was thought that it had entered a storm and been struck by lightning.

The risks and dangers of air conquest were grimly illustrated by this disaster. Airships of the semi-rigid kind had had an unhappy past. The United States had acquired a 400-foot airship, the *Roma*, from Italy in 1921, which crashed a year later killing 34 people. Again in mid-1921 the United States ordered a British Airship, the R38, which crashed on its test flight, killing 45 persons. In 1925 the 680-foot *Shenandoah*, belonging to the American Navy, disintegrated in a storm, killing fourteen officers and men. Shortly afterwards a German-built airship, the *Los Angeles*, was acquired by the United States and operated effectively for nine years. As a result the American Navy bought two large airships, with the capacity to launch scouting aircraft, from the Goodyear-Zeppelin Corporation, the *Akron* being the first to be built.

America was not the only country to have encountered trouble with airships. In 1923 the French airship *Dixmude* had been lost, 54 persons being killed, and France abandoned the development of this type of airship. Britain too had her share of disaster. In 1930 two airships had been launched, the R100 and the R101. On its way to India the R101 had crashed and burned on a French hill, killing some very senior R.A.F. officers and civil servants, ending British interest in airships. The Air Ministry decided that heavier than air machines were both safer and a better investment.

The fate of the *Akron* would have made traumatic reading for Air Commodore Fellowes, who had been Director of Airship Development in Britain between 1924 and 1929. Only a few months before the R101 crashed, he had been transferred to the Air Ministry. If matters had worked out differently he might have terminated his flying days as a passenger in the R101 on that doomed maiden voyage.

As it was Fellowes now had more pressing matters to think about. Early on the morning of 4th April he had taken off with Bonnett in the Houston Westland for a significant flight over Mount Kanchenjunga. Flying Officer Ellison with Fisher followed in the Wallace. Several hours on, Flying Officer Ellison returned to Lalbalu aerodrome, but there was no sign of the Air Commodore. Later, on the same day, alarming news reached Britain that he had had to make a crashed or forced landing some sixty miles from Purnea. Evidently his plans had gone adrift.

9 *TEMPTING FATE*

THE FIRST FLIGHT over Mount Everest had received one setback. The survey cameras had not functioned properly throughout the flight and it was to emerge after McIntyre's return from Calcutta, where the photographs were developed by the Air Survey Company, that the survey films taken were of little or no use for map-making, the photographs being inadequate on account of dust haze. The British press, in the hope that the scientific purposes of the Expedition would be fulfilled, were in favour of another flight and so were the pilots. A telegraph requesting permission for this was sent to the Prime Minister of Nepal in Kathmandu. Meteorological predictions that the good weather might not last much longer, and fear that a Monsoon might break at any time, led to a sense of urgency among the Expedition members.

Meanwhile the film director, Barkas, made it quite clear during one evening conference that more film footage of mountain peaks was needed. Fellowes, aware that the aircraft insurance gave full coverage for any flight except over Everest and that it would in any case be sensible to confirm that all the equipment was in good working order before a second Everest flight, decided to set up a flight over Kanchenjunga the next day. With

Kanchenjunga above a sea of cloud

McIntyre still in Calcutta awaiting the development of the films, the Air
Commodore decided that he and Ellison would fly the aircraft, using the
two Gaumont British photographers, Fisher and Bonnett, as observers.
Fellowes and Fisher would fly in the Houston-Westland with Ellison and
Bonnett in the Westland-Wallace. If they became separated they would
make their own way back to Purnea.

Take-off was at ten o'clock. As they climbed up through the haze,
Fellowes had trouble with a loose oxygen mask, which he had to hold up
to his face in order to check his instruments or look over the side of the
aircraft. He was determined to continue as the Expedition only had a very
limited supply of oxygen and not enough resources for another
Kanchenjunga flight. Ellison, meanwhile, was experimenting with a
perfectly fitting oxygen mask designed by McIntyre. As it had no
microphone fitted, messages to Bonnett were given from a writing pad
strapped to his knee.

At 19,000 feet they emerged from the dust haze. Behind them were the
Indian plains, with numerous rivers tumbling down through the hills from
the Himalayas. They could see the trees and vegetation over the smaller
hills, with the rivers finding their way to the plains through gorges and
valleys. In front of them Kanchenjunga loomed without any clouds.

As they came nearer a cloud formation gathered around the summit,
but they were still flying over peaks more than 20,000 feet high which had
never before been seen by man. Kanchenjunga struck them as a mass of
mountains, surrounded by scenery of limitless magnificence, with Everest

rearing up into the depths of the sky in the North-West. As they came close to Kanchenjunga its summit had suddenly become completely obscured by cloud. Ellison was leading the flight with Bonnett photographing all the time. Clearly in such circumstances it would be too dangerous to fly through cloud blind over the summit. They were so near to the cloud that they were able to fly round it, and as they did so they began to lose height so that Bonnett could take better film and photographs from a closer distance. They came very close to the mountain and experienced a serious air disturbance.

Bonnett, in the first aircraft, felt a bump so great that he thought that the Wallace would be smashed to pieces. It occurred to him that if there was a fall in engine revolution, leading to a loss of height, they would have little chance of escape amongst so many peaks. Fellowes felt the Houston Wallace twist and shake, and for a moment felt that it would go into a spin He thought that the aircraft resembled a rat being shaken vigorously by an expert terrier. To his relief they soon came out into still air.

Just after this alarming episode the two aircraft separated. On the North side of Kanchenjunga, when Ellison descended for the purpose of obtaining film and photographs, the Air Commodore in the Houston-Westland maintained his height. The Air Commodore lost sight of Ellison in the Wallace and imagined that he had returned to Lalbalu.

In fact Ellison, after enabling Bonnett to finish his cine film, climbed up searching for the Air Commodore but to no avail.[1] Fellowes, after flying for some fifteen minutes near Kanchenjunga, decided that conditions were not good enough to try to fly over its summit. He flew to the North, turning South for Lalbalu. It was then that everything began to go wrong.

The oxygen had been reaching the Air Commodore's badly fitting oxygen mask unevenly. He had found the mask a perpetual nuisance and each time he turned to look at the intruments it had slipped, causing him to lose oxygen. This made him tired, and a few minutes before he had had a shaking from the air disturbance he had been through. His mind was not functioning with its normal sharpness. He found that he could not remember which of the courses he had written down on his map was the one which he should follow, and he was now too exhausted to decipher which course was the correct one. Clouds were everywhere, and all that he could be sure of was that he was flying South.

He came down through the haze, but had no idea where he was, and could not trace his position. He was under the impression that he was flying too far to the west, and he flew along a railway line. Coming to a large open field in an area he though was uninhabited he landed the Houston Westland.

Within minutes thousands of Indians had gathered around, desperate to touch the aircraft. The engine was still running, with the propellor revolving, as the Air Commodore was keen to fly on. The starting handle which in any case needed two trained men to operate it had been left at Lalbalu to lighten the aircraft. In order to keep the Indians away from the propellor, the Air Commodore would open up the throttle. He stood up, asking the vast audience if there was anyone who understood English. At last a man appeared who pointed on the map to Shampur, a long way to the East of Lalbalu. Armed with this information the Air Commodore proceeded to turn his aircraft around for take-off, rumbling his engine to keep the crowd back. Gradually the thousands of men, women, children, donkeys, dogs and cows retired, leaving just enough room.

As soon as they were safely in the air, the petrol gauge revealed a mere ten gallons of petrol, representing some twenty-four minutes flying time, only enough to take them part of the way to Purnea. They followed the railway line to Dinajpur where there was a considerable crowd in the only landing place which could be attempted. Doing everything possible to avoid hitting anyone or anything, the Air Commodore brought the aeroplane down safely, just missing the schoolhouse and a number of trees in his second forced landing in one day. Within ten minutes some 10,000 Indians had surged around the aircraft, the first ever to have landed there and therefore a local sensation. At Dinajpur they received hospitality from the local Magistrate, whose Court had rapidly emptied on news of the landing, and from the Superintendent of Police. Both Indians were most helpful.[2]

Meanwhile back at Lalbalu Ellison had landed, with the unwelcome news that he had last seen the Air Commodore's Westland-Houston disappearing over the North of Kanchenjunga's peak. After an hour of waiting, Clydesdale and McIntyre were becoming anxious, dreading the prospect of the Air Commodore having to make a forced landing high up in the mountains. Mrs. Fellowes dealt with the crisis with firmness and efficiency. Any messages about or from her husband were to be sent to her at the Darbhanga bungalow and Clydesdale was to fly her there. Several hours later they received, to their relief, a telegram from Air Commodore Fellowes that he was at Dinajpur, some sixty miles from Purnea, without fuel or food.

Clydesdale had gathered together all the food and equipment which might be of assistance in an emergency as soon as the Air Commodore failed to return. He flew Mrs. Fellowes to Purnea, so that she would be near the telegram office, and he took off again. By the time he arrived at Dinajpur there were some 18,000 to 20,000 Indians in the vicinity of the landing site, fascinated by the flying machines. With difficulty they were persuaded to move back, to allow Clydesdale room to land. The Moth had been unable to carry enough fuel for the Houston Westland, but the Air Commodore and Fisher were very pleased to see him nonetheless, and all three of them were entertained by the Methodist Mission before spending the night in the local rest house.

Early the next morning Ellison arrived in the Puss Moth with the engineer, Cyril Pitt, and some twenty gallons of petrol. Soon the Westland had been refuelled and the Air Commodore took off in front of an enormous crowd, held back by the Indian police, to be followed by the two Moths.[3] They were reassured to learn that the survey cameras had worked well, and the flight to Kanchenjunga enabled them to check that the apparatus they had was in sufficiently good working order for a second flight to Everest.

Soon however, disturbing news arrived from Britain. The insurance company regarded the flight to Kanchenjunga as being of the same importance as a second Everest flight, and demanded payment of a further premium of £600 if another flight over Mount Everest was to be undertaken. This was a complication but, of more serious consequence, the news of the Air Commodore's mishap had reached Lady Houston and had worried her greatly. Her fears that such flights were much more dangerous than the pilots were prepared to admit seemed justified. Her first telegram which had arrived on 4th April had been full of enthusiasm but her next telegram was very different:

> The good spirit of the mountain has been kind to you and brought you success. Be content. Do not tempt the evil spirits of the mountain to bring disaster. Intuition tells me to warn you there is danger if you linger.[4]

The messages from the remainder of the members of the Expedition's Committee in Britain were similarly cautious.

On 6th April, however, they received a telegram from the Prime Minister of Nepal, conveying his hearty congratualtions on their success in flying over Everest and giving his sanction for a second flight. But despite the granting of this permission, telegrams kept coming from London demanding consultation and discouraging a second flight. To make matters worse the weather had closed in, with winds and storms, and that alone made a second flight impossible for the time being. Moreover, on 7th April, Gupta and his assistants were involved in an unfortunate accident. They had been testing wind strengths one afternoon and one of his balloons filled with hydrogen exploded, catching fire. He and his two assistants were seriously burned. The incident also denied to the pilots the necessary information on meteorology, and ruled out another flight to Everest in the immdediate future. Unless they knew about the extent of cloud formations and cloud levels, they would not be properly prepared.

The Committee in London now sent orders forbidding another flight. Air Commodore Fellowes accepted the decision and made plans to pack up and return to Britain. He then succumbed to fever, and Clydesdale, McIntyre, Blacker and Bonnett began to hatch a plot. They might, so they thought, make a second flight over Mount Everest under guise of doing something else.

Now it just so happened that Barkas, the film director, had for a long time been pressing the pilots for spectacular mountain scenery on film. The Air Commodore, from his sick bed, was persuaded to give permission for such filming, provided that the aircraft were within gliding range of Lalbalu. Barkas had earlier demanded the dropping of a smoke bomb to celebrate the first flight over Mount Everest. Clydesdale had rejected the idea at that time on the grounds that the pilots had more than enough to think about without any unnecessary distractions. Now the idea of trailing smoke for the film crew was revived. Stannic chloride was obtained from Calcutta, and was placed in a treacle tin, with two supports which could swivel spilling its contents. This device was fitted to the Westland-Houston under a lower wing. A string was attached, to be pulled during the flight, thus enabling the treacle tin to swing over, the weight of the acid forcing open the lid and the tannic acid making a smoke trail in the air.

Clydesdale and McIntyre, the two pilots

One afternoon Clydesdale took off in the Westland-Houston and at a height of between 3,000 and 4,000 feet near Lalbalu, the experiment was tried. McIntyre was following closely below and behind with Bonnett filming. The stannic chloride left a trail of smoke and Bonnett was able to obtain a film sequence, although what happened to it later the pilots never knew. At the time it was seen by many thousands of Indians, and it roused in them fears which had not been anticipated.

Already the flight over Everest had filled the Indians with fascination and admiration, but now there was suspicion. It was thought that perhaps the pilots had come to fly across the Himalayas, over Turkestan, to participate in the war between China and Japan. By word of mouth rumour spread that the members of the Expedition were beginning to practise bombing and that it would be unsafe to stay within three miles of Lalbalu aerodrome. Fortunately, the District Police Officer and the Magistrate of Purnea were quick to reassure the local residents that the purposes of the Expedition were peaceful, and that it would shortly return to Britain.[5]

Soon the pilots were once again in favour when the Rajah Banaili asked them and the aircraftsmen at Lalbalu to his race meeting on Easter Monday. The Indians, in fact, were more at risk from the members of the Expedition on runaway horses than from the aircraft. Colonel Etherton was thrown from one horse, and Shepherd's horse refused to move down the racecourse making instead for the crowd of Indians on one side. Clydesdale, on a relatively passive horse, went on to win. In return for this invitation the pilots laid on an afternoon's aerobatic display in the smaller aircraft over the Rajah Banaili's house.

The local residents began to warm again to the members of the Expedition. Purnea was a very remote area. There were a great many streams running through the countryside into the Ganges, and very few bridges crossing then. Moving by road was slow and laborious, and even if the inhabitants of Purnea had wished to be in constant contact with other towns, their remoteness would have made it extremely difficult. What the pilots were doing within their aircraft in flight was to many of the Indians quite extraordinary and they liked to have flying explained to them. Just before the first flight over Everest a former Moderator of the Church of Scotland, Dr. Graham, at his Mission School at Kalimpong, asked Clydesdale to fly over the school in his Moth. The event caused a sensation and when the children asked if they had seen something supernatural they were quickly disillusioned. Their reaction was not uncommon. Indeed some of the scenes were reminiscent of the earliest days of flying. There were even reports in the press that the tribesmen in the hills had been seen to go down on their knees when the aircraft passed overhead. There was reference to the God Krishna flying in his fiery chariot, even though members of the Expedition sought to dispel any rumours or alarm.

But the flight over Everest had caused intense interest worldwide as well and led to a number of visitors, not all of whom were invited. Some journalists from a variety of news agencies and London newspapers appeared, much to the annoyance of Shepherd who was determined that only he and *The Times* should be the recipient of unauthorised information. When one journalist persisted in visiting the aerodrome with a camera, the Air Commodore made him promise on his word of honour that he would not use anything he heard or saw there, much to the fury of Shepherd, who felt that in this respect the concession made had gone too far.

The planters around Purnea wished to be the first to celebrate the conquest of Mount Everest. Even although the pilots knew that their work was only partially completed, the planters would not be dissuaded from laying on a Victory Dinner in the Golf Clubhouse, and indeed they came from areas forty or fifty miles distant to offer the members of the Expedition their heartiest congratulations and to wish them 'God Speed' in whatever might be ahead for them. This expression of welcome and good humour refreshed the pilots for what they believed must still be done.

For the most part the members of the Expedition stayed close to the base camp, apart from one journey to the Maharajah of Darbhanga, who had so kindly lent his bungalow. Clydesdale would have liked to fly him the 100 miles from Darbhanga to Lalbalu, but the prospect of him hurtling through the air had caused distress to his mother. Instead the pilots were invited to his Palace at Darbhanga. There being no landing ground there, the Maharajah quite simply employed hundreds of Indians to make a landing strip. An area used for paddy fields was transformed into a runway for their day visit, to be converted back into fields for agricultural purposes later.

On their arrival on 13th April the pilots found the Maharajah's forty elephants present in their honour. Carriages were harnessed to the huge animals or magnificent howdahs placed on top of them, and the members of the Expedition walked as part of a parade which took them through the large estate to the Maharajah's Palace. For some of them, like Etherton,

Ancient transport mingles with the modern

The Maharajah of Darbangha's procession in honour of the expedition

Elephants and villagers beside the aircraft and hangar

there was the opportunity to climb up to the howdah, when the elephant went down on its haunches. The visitor would step on to the elephant's hind feet, hold on to the tail, pulling himself up over its behind. They were also invited to inspect the Maharajah's bodyguard, resplendent in their uniforms, with an Indian band performing from the top of one of the elephants. At the Palace a huge banquet was served to the Maharajah's guests on gold plates, in rooms filled with ornaments and differently coloured lights. The evening ending with dancing.

Next day the pilots returned to the base camp with their thoughts exclusively concentrated on secretly preparing for another flight to Mount Everest. They did not want to abandon their objective of fulfilling the purposes of the Expedition. They were only too well aware that they had just enough oxygen for one more full flight at high altitude. So they only had one more chance, and there was no scope for error.

For a good fortnight after the first flight the weather remained stormy with torrents of rain, and at times there was a risk that the aircraft might be destroyed, as the Fox Moth had been at Allahabad. However, the R.A.F. equipment was sturdy enough to offer adequate protection, even when a hailstorm descended, passing like a waterfall in a 60 mph wind. The mood of depression which the weather brought with it was accompanied by grim resolution.

During the second fortnight they came to realise that they would have to wrest what they wanted out of a set of hostile conditions. The Committee in London were opposed to a flight and the weather in the mountains was impossible. It became an accepted assumption that if they were to succeed in fulfilling their objectives, they would have to take a calculated risk. Clydesdale and McIntyre recalled their resolve, writing that "There can rarely have been a case in which a party of men set their teeth so resolutely and, saying little about it, came so unanimously to the same decision."[6]

The meteorological service arranged for a relief officer to come and assist in Gupta's place with weather reports. This officer advised that the aircraft should approach Mount Everest from the West in any subsequent flight, so that a further flight to Everest could be accomplished flying downwind. This was the view of the pilots in any case. They recognised that they would have to set a different course from their first flight, as otherwise adverse winds might cause them to run out of oxygen and petrol. Following the advice given they made a plan to fly at low level to the South West of Everest, gain height rapidly, coming towards Everest with the wind behind.

Clydesdale and McIntyre would have liked to make a trial flight, but there was insufficient oxygen to allow for any such rehearsal. They agreed not to use oxygen until absolutely necessary, and to go ahead with the second flight only if the weather conditions made it possible. "For ourselves the die had been cast. We were prepared to be judged insubordinate and to lift by our insubordination all responsibility and blame from the shoulders of the Air Commodore."[7] The secret was very well kept, and the will to succeed amongst those in the conspiracy was overwhelming.

Meanwhile, their leader remained in his sickbed, wholly unaware of these plans, but there were quite a number in on the secret. Barkas was in favour of it as he wished to have more film of Mount Everest. Blacker and Ellison were as committed as the pilots, and Fisher who had replaced Bonnett as McIntyre's observer was willing to take the risk. Shepherd of *The Times* was even prepared to risk his journalistic reputation for such a cause; and he was concerned that no other journalists should learn about it. For several days Ellison flew on a reconnaissance mission to discover the extent of the visibility above cloud levels, and found conditions to be satisfactory.

On 18th April the Air Commodore was showing signs of recovering, and that night the pilots ensured that the aircraft were fully packed with oxygen cylinders. They had received weather reports from the meteorological officer. At the height of 24,000 feet the windspeed was estimated to be 88 mph which meant from their previous experience that windlevels at 34,000 feet might be 110 mph. To fly to Everest in such a wind ran the risk of the aircraft running out of fuel, and being unable to return to Lalbalu.

Their aircraft could only fly at 120 mph so their course had to be charted with especial care by McIntyre. They would fly 120 miles North West at the low level of 3,000 feet, then North climbing to 18,000 feet, with enough fuel and oxygen to overcome the winds and complete the survey flight, with vertical photographs of the ground to the South of Everest.

At dawn on 19th April the pilots, hoping that the weather would not let them down, tiptoed out of the Bungalow, while the Air Commodore was asleep. They were slightly concerned at the mass of clouds seen by their light scouting Moth flown by Ellison, but in their view this was no time for second thoughts. At the aerodrome the cameras were soon installed. McIntyre, annoyed at the failure of his vertical camera on the first flight, had dismantled it, cleaned it, and adjusted it, checking it over with great care.

By 7.45 a.m. they were ready and at 7.50 a.m. the throttles were opened and the two aircraft raced down the runway. As they saw it they had come to India to make a complete success of their Expedition, and they could only be satisfied with the very best results. They were engaged in doing precisely what Lady Houston had asked them not to do. They were pressing their luck, placing their own lives lightly in the balance. They were, quite simply, tempting fate.

10 MAGNIFICENT INSUBORDINATION

As THEIR AIRCRAFT gathered speed down the landing strip, the pilots and crew were aware that their only defence would be that they had managed to crown the efforts of the Expedition with total success. They knew that at a height of 34,000 feet the wind levels might run at about 120 mph, in fact at a speed equal to that of their aircraft, so aeroplanes flying into such a headwind would remain stationary and be unable to make any progress towards Everest. They would have to take into account the tremendous downcurrents, unless they kept well above the mountain.

Within seconds the two aircraft were airborne in a cloudy sky. They flew towards Chiuribote, where the Maulung Khola joins the Sun Kosi river. The pilots had chosen this site to the South West of Mount Everest and it was their intention to reach it in about an hour. Owing to the very strong winds over Everest they would fly to the West to get the wind behind them, so that they could obtain the necessary height to complete the survey, moving with the wind-drift. At first they found the wind at low levels came from the East, and with the wind behind them the aircraft surged forward.

Soon they crossed the Kosi river, and noticed that the clouds were not continuous. If they flew up into the clouds to get above them, they might

The infra-red photograph taken of Mount Everest over a hundred miles away

be unable to see Chiuribote, and whilst climbing through them the aircraft might collect ice on the wings and fuselage. This would add to the weight of the aircraft, making it impossible to gain greater height than the summit of Everest. On the other hand, in order to leave as little to chance as possible, they needed to gain height.

Clydesdale chose what he thought was the biggest gap in the clouds and began the ascent. The cloud proved to be infinitely deeper than he had imagined, and all that was visible was a small portion of the Indian plains directly under them. At the height of 18,000 feet they emerged, coming out above the clouds with a magnificent view. In Clydesdale's words:

> We had the finest sight of the whole Expedition. For a distance of about 80 miles the sea of almost unbroken cloud stretched to the line of the mountains. The white cloud-tips seen in the sunshine billowed away into the distance like cotton-wool packing, out of which the still brighter white of the ice cliffs raised its ultimate challenge to the sky and gave it a particularly deep shade of blue. There was none of the gloom of the drab dust-haze about this prospect.
>
> Cloud and mountain cast back the flare of the sun towards the sky and we found ourselves in a world not only of brilliant reflections and highlights, but of marvellous clear visibility. Kanchenjunga was far away but Everest and Makalu stood out as the dominating features of a vast mountain landscape and looked absolutely colossal. . . .
>
> Never have I found a scene set on such a scale. Once again we could see far beyond the mountains which were our aim, and again the picture produced a definitely intoxicating effect.[1]

Up until this moment they had not used oxygen, in order to be sure that they would be able to complete the mission which included taking vertical photographs of the Southern walls of Mount Everest. If they were to go on, a decision would have to be made as to whether the remainder of the oxygen should be used.

Although much of the Himalayan foothills and countryside were covered with cloud, it appeared that it might be possible to photograph over the last twenty miles. They began to climb more rapidly, aiming Westwards. At the height of 21,000 feet they turned on the remainder of their oxygen, knowing this to be their last chance. Within a few minutes their oxygen would all be gone.

They were climbing with all possible speed, making progress towards Mount Everest, but experiencing considerable drift as the tremendous wind force swept them Eastwards. They had emerged completely from the clouds at a height of over 31,000 feet, some twenty miles from Everest. Immediately the electrical controls of the survey cameras were turned on, so that they would automatically take photographs of the mountains, glaciers and ridges underneath every fifteen seconds.

Although their course was plotted well to the West of Everest there was a risk that they might be forced on to the Eastern side. Clydesdale had changed course on a number of occasions in order to maintain a Westerly direction when he experienced a nasty incident. He saw that the plug for heating his oxygen had dropped out of its socket. If moisture gathered into the system, it might soon freeze, thus preventing oxygen passing through the valve to the oxygen mask. If this were allowed to happen the consequences would be fatal.

He tried to insert the plug into the socket but it would not remain there. He informed Blacker of this predicament by means of the rough and ready telephone system. Within seconds a screwdriver was produced from the observer's cabin and handed through to the pilot's open cockpit. The two legs of the plug were parted further with the use of the screwdriver. To their immense relief it began to operate again.

While this distraction with the heating plug was taking place the drift of the hurricane had forced the Houston-Westland to the West, and it had come closer to the Wallace. McIntyre took the opportunity to manoeuvre from the right to the left, so as to give his observer Fisher the opportunity to film the Wallace with Mount Everest in front of it, only about twelve miles away. The two pilots had previously agreed not to cross the summit of Everest, as a concession to the Everest Committee at home, and to come back with a full vertical survey of the mountainous terrain just South of Everest's summit. In any case the tumultuous wind was a source of great concern to Clydesdale:

> To my eye the drift appeared far greater than anything I had ever experienced before. The snowfields so comparatively close, were slipping away sideways at a furious rate, and although the vertical camera had been set going, I could not resist the temptation to turn dead into the wind. Then I found the machine seemed to make no progress whatsoever. It just hovered stationary until I turned back on my course.[2]

His impression of a very high wind was confirmed by the sight of the plume of Everest, streaming "horizontally away to the East like the steam of a giant railway engine".[3] This time it was larger and longer, at least six miles in length, covering half the distance between Everest and Makalu. Chamlang could be seen on the right. Clydesdake was flying at 34,000 feet, but the wind had swept him off course. If he were to fly over Everest, the only way he could do it would be to fly through the plume before reaching the summit.

He had already flown over the summit twice on his first flight, and the memories of approaching Everest on its lee side, with its mighty downdraught were fresh in his mind. This time the position was again a dangerous one. While the aircraft were flying higher than before, the power of the hurricane wind was approximately twice as powerful as it had been on the earlier flight.

He flew on until he was within three-and-a-half miles of Everest's summit, and there he felt it would be wise to turn. All this time Blacker in the rear cabin had been working with energetic enthusiasm. He had had a struggle with the survey camera, as one of its clamping screws had seized and the invaluable screwdriver was used to release it. He was taking photographs of the ranges and ridges running South-West from Everest,

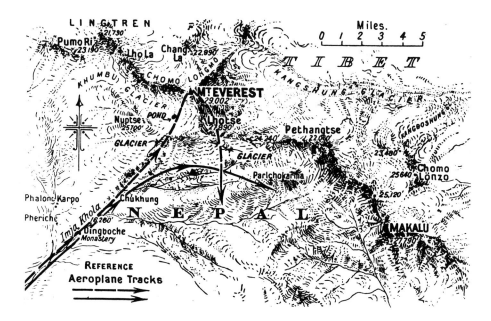

Map showing the course of the two aircraft on the second flight

and which had never been photographed before. He concentrated on helping the survey camera to function, leaning over the side of the cabin to take photographs and to focus the cine camera on the most stupendous sights. He also had a small Kodak cine camera and his attention was divided among all four cameras. The supervision of the fixed camera in the floor of the cabin took place each few seconds. In between Blacker would jump up, reloading the Williamson P14 camera, uncovering the slide, setting the camera, selecting the view, steadying it and taking the photograph. The slide was then quickly covered and deposited in a slide box to keep out the light.

His description of his last close encounter with Mount Everest was vivid:

Everest lay straight before us and great cliff-bound valleys streaked with snowfields were clear beneath us. . . . The pilot handled the machine with that hardihood and surpassing accuracy which filled me now, as ever, with complete confidence.

Soon we flew once again over the cliffs of the South Peak scarred with its huge triangular crags. We came close once more to Everest which had lost none of its entrancing beauty. The machine circled serenely, unmindful of the hurricane blast to which the six mile long plume from Everest's summit bore witness. I photographed incessantly, striving always to remember the gaps of the first flight and to make them good for science.

Now we were over the spurs of Everest and now over the peak of Makalu and the yet untrodden tangled ranges to the South East. Meanwhile the mountain came ever closer, bare and clear in the wonderful atmosphere and free from cloud, except for its great plume, now bigger than ever. In the crystal clear weather I was delighted at the view over the great Khumbu glacier and the terrific ridges which bound it. Again to the West, for an immense distance, stretched a chain of countless peaks, while in front to the East the great range continued, broken slightly by the Arun Gorge, then sweeping round to the huge mass of Kanchenjunga. . . . On we swept, veering a little more to the North East to skirt the Southern declivities and to shape a course practically on Makalu.

McIntyre in the Wallace, behind and to the left saw the leading machine as it wheeled in the sky. "It slipped away downwind in an incredibly short space of time and it seemed only a few seconds before it was a tiny black speck away beyond Makalu."[4]

McIntyre had already edged over to the left, keeping as accurate a course as possible for the summit. He could not help remembering that on the first flight Clydesdale had flown over the summit twice. In his case, with Bonnett unconscious in the observer's cabin of the Wallace, he had been anxious to lose height after clearing the summit in order to hasten Bonnett's recovery. Now it seemed that he too had a reasonable prospect of clearing the summit of Everest for a second time, and whatever the orders from home the temptation was too great for him. For a moment he was undecided as to whether he should follow his leader or to continue his photographic survey to Everest. He resolved to push on to the mountain.

He set course more to the left, but with the hurricane bearing down on him, made very slow progress. The drift swept him towards the summit of Everest.

There on my right was the enormous pinnacle, the bright morning sun glinting on the frozen snow and throwing into strong relief the great rock faces, some of them a sheer 8,000 feet or more.

The next fifteen minutes was a grim struggle. The altimeter showed 34,000 feet. The menacing peak with its enormous plume whirling and streaking away to the South-East at 120 miles an hour, appeared to be almost underneath us but refused to get right beneath. After what seemed an interminable time, it disappeared below the nose of the aircraft. I determined to hold the compass course until I gauged we were just over the mountain. Petrol was getting low and I knew there would not be sufficient to go beyond.

We appeared to be stationary. I cast quick, anxious glances behind and below to see if we had passed over. Then suddenly there was a terrific bump—just one terrific impact such as one might receive flying over an explosives factory as it blew up.

It felt as if the wings should break off at the roots, but there was no nasty cracking noise such as would have denoted structural failure. A hurried look round showed every wire taut. There was no sign of slackness anywhere. We were thankful for the marvellous strength of our aeroplane. The bump was a relief in a way, as it indicated the summit and was the signal for a careful, gentle turn to the right to settle down on our predetermined compass course for home.[5]

Meanwhile Clydesdale had flown over Makalu, to obtain a series of photographs which overlapped, connecting Everest's Southern face with Makalu. Having flown over its peak, he turned to the right, made for Chamlang and then pointed towards Mount Everest and the full strength of the hurricane. Blacker thought that the aircraft was actually being blown backwards, and as they seemed to be making little or no headway, Clydesdale turned once again. They flew over Chamlang in the direction of the Arun Valley with its fast-flowing river, surrounded by pine forests and sandbanks.

The screwdriver was being used to reload the cine camera when it slipped from Blacker's hand through the floor hatch. The last that was seen of it was the flash of sunlight glinting from it as it plunged downwards to Nepal. Within a few more seconds not only the oxygen but also the film had been used up, and they descended through the clouds near Forbesganj, landing at Lalbalu after three-and-a-half hours of flight.

McIntyre was following some fifteen minutes behind. He came to the end of his survey film opposite the Western mountain wall of Makalu, passed the glaciers of Chamlang, descended through the cloud and came out over the foothills of the Himalayas, seeing dried-up river beds. He recognised the River Kosi and the village, Dharan, over which he had flown in a tropical thunderstorm a few days before. He flew the last fifteen miles, landing not long afterwards. There he found Clydesdale and an extremely anxious Air Commodore, who had been waiting for them.

He did not have to be told what had happened. When the pilots had taken off, after making the most extensive preparations, the mechanics and aircraftmen had sensed that a major flight had been planned. Some ninety minutes after they departed, Air Commodore Fellowes arrived, and expressed great surprise that they had not returned. After a further thirty minutes he began to ask searching questions, and soon learned that all of the remaining oxygen had been taken as well as the vertical cameras and equipment, and that the tanks of the two aircraft had been filled with fuel. For the next sixty minutes he was in a state of grave anxiety. On his shoulders rested the responsibility for the well-being of the members of the Expedition and of the aircraft.

When first one aircraft and then another reappeared he was so relieved that he almost forgot to be angry. Not only had explicit orders been challenged, but it seemed that the pilots had been wholly successful in the process. It would be some hours before the results could be assessed. Aircraftman Fraser was working in the dark room to develop the photographs, adding ice to them so that they would not be damaged.

Clydesdale attempted to appease the Air Commodore, making it clear that both pilots sought to avoid any publicity on the subject. Their wish

The Wallace over the Himalayas

was not to be granted. The most that the leader of the Expedition would agree to was that his report would be delayed until the next day, by which time the quality of the survey photographs would be known. Shepherd of *The Times* refused to agree to unconditional silence. He had promised to send to his office a coded telegram mentioning that the second flight to Mount Everest had taken place. He would request the delaying of publication, but if news of what had happened leaked, he would tell the whole story.

The suspense of waiting to see if the photographs would come out was intense, and Blacker found relief in flying up to 21,000 feet in the afternoon, without oxygen, to take infra-red photographs. By the time he returned he was thrilled to see the results. That afternoon, evening and night the photographs were fully developed. Both aeroplanes had obtained many shots whose quality was excellent. They included two continuous survey strips from the South of Mount Everest to Makalu. The overlaps were complete, so the remaining task before the Expedition of photographing the apparently inaccessible country from an extreme height had been accomplished.

The Westland Wallace and the Houston Westland, two of last pioneering aircraft in the world some years before the space age

On 21st April the news of their success received thorough coverage in the world press. Under the headline "Success on all Points", *The Times* wrote that, "The second flight to Everest, which took place yesterday, may well be described by historians of great achievements as a piece of magnificent insubordination. Made in uninsured aeroplanes and without authority from home it was carried through with the greatest success and has yielded results of the highest scientific value".[6] There was much enthusiasm for the fact that the survey photographs would provide geographers with the means of accurate mapping of a part of the Himalayas, and that the other photographs would give a dramatic impression of the gigantic scale and rugged bleakness of Everest and the Himalayas, where men could never be more than temporary intruders. There was a sense of awe that aircraft had achieved results which men unaided could never have aspired to achieve.

Marshal of the Royal Air Force, Sir John Salmond, Chief of the Air Staff, sent a telegram: "My sincere congratulations on successful completion of difficult survey flight". This indicated that the Royal Air Force accepted the verdict of *The Times* on 24 April:[7]

> Forbidden to make the second flight, they concerted one of those acts of constructive insubordination which cannot be justified until they have succeeded, and which, when they have succeeded, need no justification.
>
> The second air journey was the more forgiveable because the ban which the airmen disregarded was for their own safety, and they have returned unharmed.
>
> It was forgiveable, too, because it was carried out not for the glorification of the flyers, who had glory enough, but as a debt to science.[8]

Far from being critical many of the papers, like the *Huddersfield Examiner,* went so far as to say in their headlines and articles, that never since the day that Admiral Lord Nelson was sent a signal to withdraw at Copenhagen, and had placed his telescope to his blind eye, had there been a case of such "Magnificent Insubordination".[9]

11 HOMECOMING

THE PILOTS AND observers felt a professional satisfaction that the scientfic purpose of the Expedition, to show that aircraft equipped with cameras could acquire otherwise unattainable knowledge over the world's highest mountain, had been accomplished. They had established that air photography over mountainous territory, including the highest point of the world's surface, could be used for map-making purposes and they had brought back specimen strip, which would reveal the physical features of Everest's Southern face. The procedure they had adopted had been to obtain overlapping photographs from a number of points, whose latitude and longitude were known.

The Williamson Automatic Eagle III Survey Camera had completed the job well on the second occasion. On the first flight nothing of value was recorded on the strips. On the second flight Clydesdale's camera took a continuous strip of the six to seven miles West of Makalu and there Blacker's camera jammed. McIntyre's photographs over the South of Everest, the peak and the East, taken by Fisher, ran out of film at the same area in which the camera in Clydesdale's aircraft had stopped functioning. The two strips of film overlapped and they were sent to Colonel Macleod and Lieutenant Salt of the Geographical Section of the British War Office. Maps were made from them in due course, showing that existing maps were incomplete and inaccurate. Various glaciers had not been recorded and in one case a glacier was shown between two ridges which had previously been mistaken as one ridge, an error easily made when mountains and cliffs can only be witnessed from afar.

Just above Lhotse II at 18,090 feet appeared a lake on the outskirts of Everest. This discovery suggested that the lake derived some heat from a volcanic source in the earth. McIntyre wanted to call it Loch Everest, but the naming of places with British names was a sensitive matter, and nothing came of his suggestion.[1]

As well as the survey work there were the photographs taken by the observers, when they worked, encumbered with oxygen masks, goggles, heated suits and cameras, with their head and shoulders protruding from their cabin in the slipstream of the aircraft. Of the eighty photographs taken 43 were selected for detailed examination by the Royal Geographical Society, some of which would be published in their *Journal.*

Their work had revealed a great deal about the Southern side of Mount Everest. Clydesdale and McIntyre summed up their emotions in a few words:

Our Expedition was concerned particularly with the science of flight, of geography and exploration. No man can come closer to the great peaks without acknowledging a sense of awe, and understanding something of the fascinations they hold. . . . We saw the mountain on both occasions in high sunshine when there were few shadows to shroud her mystery. In softer lights one might expect to feel something of the romance of these enormous masses of rock and ice.

Something of the mystery had been overcome and something of the unknown had been revealed; yet the Mistress of the World remains remote, immense and magnificent. The best that we could bring back was but a faint impression of her dignity and beauty.[2]

At the time it was hoped that the photographs they had taken would be of assistance to Hugh Ruttledge's climbing expedition, but it was not to be. Appalling weather conditions and ferocious winds prevented his expedition succeeding, and it would be twenty years before men would set foot on Everest's summit. As it happened one of the photographs taken by the aircraft of Clydesdale and McIntyre proved to be very useful to the successful expedition led by Colonel John Hunt who wrote:

The prints of photographs taken during the flight over the mountain in 1933 were handed to me when I arrived at the Royal Geographical Society to take over the leadership of the 1953 Everest Expedition, in October 1952; I think they had been sent to Eric Shipton by the Duke of Hamilton.

The shots showing the South-East ridge, particularly the final section between the South summit and the top, were particularly interesting. The Swiss Guide Raymond Lambert and Tenzing had not climbed higher than about 28,100 feet on that ridge in May 1952, so the last 700 feet or so to the South summit, and onwards to the final peak of Everest, was all unknown ground.

There was much speculation among us about a 'step', shown clearly on one of the photos; it looked steep, if not vertical, and we guessed that it might be as

Photograph of Mount Everest's south east ridge, of value to the 1953 Everest mountaineering expedition

much as 40 or 50 feet in height. When Hillary and Tenzing climbed Everest on 29th May 1953 they found this to be a difficult obstacle, which involved a jamming technique between a short rock wall and a mass of snow which had become partly detached from the wall on the eastern face of the mountain. From subsequent reports, I gather that the problem varies from year to year, depending on the snow conditions on the ridge.

On return from our Expedition I paid a call at Lennoxlove, the home of the Duke of Hamilton, to thank him for his valuable help. I have kept these photographs ever since, with my other planning documents of the climb.[3]

The most immediate results of the Everest flights were that lessons had been learnt, which would be of benefit to others at that stage in the development of aviation. First of all it would have been an advantage if they had been able to fly with a prevailing wind behind them. With the gift of hindsight they might have seen more of the Himalayas and photographed more if they had used another landing strip to the North-West, giving them the opportunity to fly over Everest downwind, landing to refuel in the South-East before returning to base. Alternatively in the future, stronger more powerful aircraft could be built, capable of flying faster, higher and for greater distances, and a complete survey of the Himalayas would be possible in favourable conditions. Much knowledge had been acquired about meteorological conditions and the high winds at extreme altitudes over the mountains. The vertical currents, caused by winds passing rapidly over the peak of a mountain, were similar to those passing over smaller mountains, the difference being in degrees and not in character.

Secondly, virtually everyone involved was disgruntled with the flying equipment. The heavy oxygen apparatus, helmet and goggles could easily be disarranged if the pilot or observer moved his head, and at different times all of them experienced difficulty with it. As for the heated suits, the plugs and wires could become entangled or disconnected and this precluded the pilots or observers from making sudden movements. Overall the equipment was inefficient and clumsy and it would need to be completely redesigned. These would be improved in due course, and of course enclosed pressurised cockpits would make the cumbersome oxygen masks and goggles unnecessary. After the three flights the observers had looked more tired than the pilots due to the fact that they had to stand up in an open cockpit in the slipstream and manipulate heavy cameras. If their cabin had been enclosed, their task would have been easier.

Thirdly, the survey and cine cameras gave some trouble, and if it had been possible to keep them at a constant temperature, they would have functioned better and would not have ceased working. Here too there was room for improvement.

Fourthly, the supercharged Bristol Pegasus engines had been up to the task of carrying the two heavily laden aircraft over Everest, but soon there would be a need for more powerful engines to ascend higher and for more than one engine in case one failed. It was also noted that in the vicinity of high mountains a pilot should closely observe his instruments so as to obtain the necessary height to avoid downdraughts. Flying over Mount Everest had been just technically possible, and one day commercial airlines would benefit from the experience and fly aircraft with passengers at the same heights.[4]

It is easy to place the Everest flight within its purely historical perspective. The Wright brothers had flown from Kitty Hawk Field just thirty years before, and, within thirty years of the Everest flight, commercial flying would become a popular means of commercial transport, in which much of the British population would participate, flying at altitudes well above Everest. As a result sea travel by passenger lines became reduced in scope. Within forty years man would set foot on the moon and pioneering came to be reserved for visits into space.

The Everest flight came roughly at the very end of the first phase of heavier-than-air flying. Indeed it was virtually the last significant pioneer event of that period. The design and equipment of aircraft had not basically changed from the early years of the first World War. The cockpits were open and the undercarriage could not be retracted. The airscrew was solid wood without variable pitch control, let alone constant speed. There was no radio equipment to receive or transmit, no flaps or slots on the wings and the oxygen supply and blend of flying instruments and navigation equipment all were of primitive design. There had been no previous experience as to what would be required for the cameras or indeed for clothing on an operational flight of that kind.

The flight was the first time a task had been carried out in such circumstances, a venture which tested the equipment to its very limits. Since that time aviation has developed over a very wide front, in which a multitude of ideas have been tested by the iron discipline of trial and error. At a period of development the Everest flight was a very fundamental test of the design and equipment of the time. In few areas of human activity is it more appropriate to remember that the mountains of the future become the molehills of the past.

Naturally, after the second flight to Mount Everest, the pilots thought that the work was completed, but Geoffrey Barkas, the film director, wanted more film to complete his documentary "Wings over Everest" for posterity. He persuaded Blacker and Etherton to accompany him to Darjeeling.

The film party travelled by car from Purnea to Siliguri where they ascended on the small mountain railway. Everywhere they were surrounded by vegetation, bamboo and tea trees. Eventually Darjeeling revealed itself high up on a ridge. There they were entertained by Sir John Anderson, the Governor of Bengal, at Government House, and they could see the Himalayas more than forty miles away "With Kanchenjunga towering above the rest like a King in silver armour enthroned among his barons."[5]

1933. The climbers approaching Mount Everest have to wait 20 years before men would set foot on the summit

They spent much of their time shooting scenes from Tiger hill, of the snowy peaks thronging the horizon. This constituted the final part of the film, which began with Blacker and Etherton surveying Mount Everest and expressing the hope that one day men might be able to fly over it. It showed Lady Houston in her sick-bed, consenting to finance the undertaking, and it told the story as to how the machines were assembled and made ready for the flight. The conferences between the pilots and observers, the clothing they wore and their equipment, were all included in the footage shot.

The film on the ascent over the Indian plains, towards the mountains, over the foothills, gave a clear impression of the dangers if engine or oxygen failure occurred. It revealed the mistake of Bonnett in treading on his oxygen tube and his presence of mind in bandaging it with a handkerchief before dropping down unconscious through lack of oxygen.

Clydesdale had reservations about the film, since it omitted the part played by Gupta and the meteorologists, made no mention of the help from the Maharajahs, and in his view did not concentrate enough on the scientific purposes of the Expedition. Barkas on the other hand intended the film to be an enthralling account of a great achievement and of the tenacity which had led to its success. Thus it was that secrets of the world, which had been seen by a handful of men at first hand would soon be seen by countless others. *The Times* had sent a telegram that it intended to give a lunch in honour of the members of the Expedition after they arrived in Britain.

Blacker was now anxious to return home and booked on a Dutch aircraft, flying West from Calcutta. Clydesdale, being grateful to the Rajah of Banaili for his hospitality, asked Ellison to give the eminent Indian a ride in the Moth. The Rajah had expressed the hope that he could return to Purnea by air, as he had never flown, and he felt that his many employees would like to see him do so. He was a large heavy man and could only get into the Moth cockpit with difficulty, and by the time that they landed at Purnea, on 21st April, Ellison found it impossible to remove him from the aircraft. It is a known fact that nervous apprehension in someone flying for the first time can cause swelling. It was about half an hour before he could be assisted from the cockpit, without damage to the aircraft or himself. Even so he was delighted to have had experience of flying, especially in front of many thousands of his own employees.

On return to Purnea the film and equipment were carefully packed away, and the remaining members of the Expedition made ready to leave. Clydesdale and Ellison took off on 24th April on the journey to Karachi, flying the Wallace and the Houston Westland respectively. They took with them the two engineers, Pitt and Burnard, an aircraftman and Shepherd, the last of whom wanted a lift to Delhi, before making off to the North West Frontier to spend a few days with the Royal Air Force there.

In the morning sunlight they had their last view of the awe-inspiring mountains, as they embarked on a bumpy journey, flying through much turbulence. On 25th April they flew on to Jodhpur. There they learnt that the Delhi Flying Club's Moth, carrying the mail to Karachi, had had to make a forced landing after collision with a kite. Clydesdale agreed to carry the mail on to Karachi the next day, a task for which he received sincere thanks.

Back at Lalbalu, McIntyre was flying the Gipsy III Moth, giving rides to all members of the Expedition who had not seen Mount Everest. Flights had been given to the Police and to the Headmen in the villages. Some of their expressions had been somewhat amusing as they sat with faces set, eyes staring and hands clutching the sides of the aeroplane. At the same time McIntyre was sending off the remaining stores and was waiting for Etherton, who was journeying to thank the Maharajah of Darbhanga for his hospitality and making courtesy calls. A day or so later McIntyre and Etherton, in the Gipsy III Moth, and Air Commodore Fellowes with Mrs Fellowes in the Puss Moth, took off from Lalbalu on the way to Lucknow. They had a last look at the mountains with their matchless beauty and, in the glittering brilliance emitted from the summit, they flew away from the vast mountain ranges, over the Indian plains.

At Lucknow the British Commissioner, Darling, met them and showed them the town where men, women and children had been under siege during the Indian Mutiny, virtually starving and almost beyond hope when they heard the skirl of the bagpipes in the distance heralding the coming of the Highlanders and the Relief of Lucknow. On leaving there they flew to the small landing ground at Dholpur, having already received an invitation to stay with Lieutenant Colonel Sir Udai Bhan Singh Lokindra Bahadur, the Maharajah Rana of Dholpur, who was very interested in aviation.

McIntyre would have liked to stay with Etherton at the Maharajah's Palace, but he remembered the destruction of the Fox Moth in the storm at Allahabad, some 250 miles away, and decided to stay with the aircraft on the landing ground. He slept on top of a sentry box, and the next morning was roused by the flapping of a great swarm of birds streaming above him. He soon discovered that this time the anticipated tropical storm had struck elsewhere, and these birds were escaping from its path. After half an hour the flocks decreased in numbers, leaving the stragglers in their wake.

After leaving Dholpur they flew North to Agra, and from there towards Jodhpur, when they encountered a tremendous storm, the fearsome nature of which shook Etherton to the core, however impressed he was with McIntyre's skill as a pilot:

> We had risen high above the Agra plain, when in the far distance a brown wall appeared that seemed to rise out of the earth. The day was becoming black as night and full of moaning voices; nothing was visible except a dark rampart of storm advancing to sweep everything out of its path.
>
> Making a hurried circuit in the darkness, we started a race for life against the oncoming typhoon . . . we rocked along, partly under our own propulsion,

partly urged on irresistibly from behind. Gusts of the typhoon caught up and leaped over us like devils playing at leapfrog.

Over the side of the cockpit was the Agra Aerodrome, and almost at once the aeroplane was gliding towards a walled enclosure. . . . The storm was upon us again, reaching such a pitch of wild intensity that for a minute or two the machine seemed as though it would be swept away into the air. . . .

We carried up large boulders and did what we could to anchor the aeroplane; then we held on to the wings, one on each side, hanging on for dear life, determined that the little plane should not be dragged away and torn to pieces.[6]

The Air Commodore and his wife had fared slightly better. He had tried to fly above the storm, and then attempted to go round it; nevertheless, they had experienced a very rough passage. On the next day McIntyre and Etherton joined them at Jodhpur after a calm flight in the glow of the sun. There they were welcomed by the Maharajah of Jodhpur, whose family had enjoyed a warm relationship with the British Crown for many years. The Maharajah's Uncle, Sir Pertab Singh, had fought in France in 1914 with the Jodhpur Lancers and had worn in his turban a miniature of Queen Victoria, set in pearls. In 1922, much to his delight, he had been warmly congratulated by the Prince of Wales when the Jodhpur team had won the Rutlam Polo Cup. The young Maharajah shared his great enthusiasm for horses and polo as well as for flying. He believed that man had achieved mastery of the horse, but had yet to gain full mastery of the air.

After Jodhpur, they flew on to Udaipur, a place of outstanding beauty, where they were the guests of the Maharana who refused to allow them to pay for the cost of their board and lodging. There Etherton was very struck by the improbability of what he saw:

The beauty of the spot really consisted in the wealth of water and islands, each adorned by a marble palace or temple. With its palm trees and blue lakes the place is really a little bit of Italy that has wandered off into the tropics and got lost. One has the feeling that Udaipur is not India at all, but a piece of Eastern enchantment stolen from the West, that may one day wake up and remember it does not really exist in a modern world.[7]

Only a few miles away from the town, a somewhat different picture emerged. In thick jungle was a fort from which grain was fed to wild pigs which came scrambling out of their lairs to fight for food. Here too, combats were held in an arena between tiger and pig. The tiger would be entrapped and the wild pig, selected for strength, would be captured. They would then be put together in the arena to fight. In the ferocious gladitorial battle that followed, more often than not the pig would win.

It was a bright morning early in May when Air Commodore Fellowes and McIntyre left Udaipur, their aeroplanes circling overhead, dipping in salute, before flying to Karachi. Etherton chose to return by train and ship.

At Karachi the Air Commodore, Mrs Fellowes and McIntyre were joined by Ellison. Together they flew the three Moths back towards Britain by a different route after Baghdad, leaving Karachi on 6th May. At each landing McIntyre and Ellison changed cockpits, each taking turns at flying along a carefully navigated route.

They reached Bandar Abbas in Persia where they stayed the night in a nearby hotel. There they had a minor complication as Persia had no paper money, and it was illegal to take silver coinage out of the country. Before they could depart McIntyre went to the bank to cash a traveller's cheque for five pounds, so that he could pay the hotel bill. Ellison went to the landing ground to complete a service on the aircraft, and was astonished to see McIntyre arrive with the Air Commodore and Mrs Fellowes, carrying in each hand two sacks of coins, genuine silver and most of them as large as the old British crown or five-shilling piece.

The next night stop should have been in Baghdad, but as a dust storm was blowing over the town, they diverted to Hinaida in Iraq on 7th May and stayed the night in the Mess at the RAF depot after eleven hours flying that day. Early on 8th May Ellison flew solo to Baghdad to obtain customs clearance in and out of Iraq and returned to Hinaida to join the others.

They then departed from Deir-Ez-Zor in Syria and landed to find that the aerodrome was partly used by the French Air Force. The French officers gave them a very warm welcome and showed them around hangars full of very clean and polished fighter aircraft. As the French Government could not afford to purchase petrol none of their aircraft had been flown for months. Not disheartened by this bizarre information, the pilots walked into the bazaar to hire a man with two donkeys, which could be loaded up with four gallon cans of petrol, to refuel the aircraft. This interlude caused some merriment amongst Fellowes, McIntyre and Ellison, as they could not get over the spectacle of magnificent fighter aircraft, quite unable to fly. After refuelling they took off and reached Aloppo after nightfall.

On 9th May they flew on to Istanbul via Konia in Turkey, where they stopped for fuel and were delayed by an official who was quite unable to read, write or speak English. He refused to sign the regulation Customs Clearance Certificate, and for once McIntyre lost his natural calm and became very cross. They decided to pay no attention to this official, and took off without permission.

At Istanbul they were met by the representative of the local Castrol Oil Company who was extremely helpful. Customs proved to be very difficult, since McIntyre said he had taken no film of consequence over Turkey. Unhappily a roll of film was found in his suitcase, which had been turned out by the officials in the hangar. The officials demanded the Leica camera which had been left in McIntyre's cockpit, and it was traced and found to have a roll of film in it. These rolls were confiscated.

The representative of the Castrol Oil Company took the party into a hotel in the town, and on the next day the pilots spent much of their time with the British Ambassador at the Embassy, ending up at a large dinner in their honour. Early on 11th May Castrol Oil Company's employee had arranged to show them around the city. Instead he warned the pilots that he had received a tip-off that the customs official had developed McIntyre's film and was very suspicious about the aerial photographs he had taken. He advised them to leave Turkey as soon as possible. They went down to the airport, driven by their friend, and the three aircraft took off illegally, without even clearing customs, and proceeded to Sofia in Bulgaria.

On arrival at Sofia they checked in at a hotel, and Ellison and McIntyre mentioned their wish to see the town and dine out. The Air Commodore and Mrs Fellowes were reluctant to leave the hotel. They had kept a close eye on the two younger pilots up until that point, and expressed their preference for them to remain in the hotel. McIntyre and Ellison went up in the lift first, noted the position of their rooms and ran down the stairs, leaving a short note for the Air Commodore that they would see him for breakfast at 07.00 hours. They asked for it to be delivered in fifteen minutes time.

McIntyre and Ellison found a very interesting restaurant, at which nobody seemed to speak any English or French. The manager appeared and, realising that he had two British guests, went off and returned with the drummer from the orchestra, who spoke excellent English. He explained that he was to spend the evening with McIntyre and Ellison, with the Manager's compliments, as it was such a rare occurrence for him to have British guests. From him they learnt much about Bulgaria.

At breakfast next day the Air Commodore made no mention of their evening out, and they flew on to Budapest in Hungary amidst rain and low clouds, the flying time being four hours and fifty minutes. That evening, after seeing the town, the Air Commodore and Mrs Fellowes allowed McIntyre and Ellison to take them out to an excellent restaurant where a full string orchestra played. On 13th May they left Budapest at midday and flew the whole route to Vienna up the blue Danube, flying at tree top level in order to keep below the clouds and to see the scenery, landing at Wein on the Northern side of the city. That evening the group enjoyed another night out, listening to an Austrian string orchestra.

On 14th May they flew on to Nuremberg amidst bad weather, and there the British airline representative warned them that now that the Nazi Party had come to power in Germany there were a lot of people giving the Hitler salute and saying "Heil Hitler". In their view it was advisable to steer clear of crowds giving the Hitler salute, as they could become physically agressive towards people who did not return it. As well as receiving this warning they noticed that the Airport officials were all dressed in smart green uniforms, and had a distinct military bearing. They were most interested to learn that there was a great deal of club flying at Nuremberg and realised that there was a purpose behind it. Under the Versailles

Treaty Germany was not allowed to rearm beyond a certain level, but these flying clubs were obviously receiving funds from the State, and the German pilots of these clubs were openly boasting that under the disguise of flying club activity they would one day became the central core of the Luftwaffe. After spending the night the British Party left Nuremberg, with an uneasy feeling about the intoxicated enthusiasm the German flying club pilots had for the new Nazi regime. They had cause, for Britain and Germany would be at war before the decade was over.

On 15th May they had intended to fly via Brussels to Heston, but due to very bad weather conditions, they landed at Darnstadt. After waiting for three hours for the weather to clear, they were able to complete their journey, arriving at Heston at 19.15 hours, some ten days after leaving Karachi, their flying time being 55 hours and twenty minutes. At Heston they were met by a crowd of well-wishers.[8]

Fellowes, Ellison and McIntyre arrive at Heston on 15 May

In the meantime as there had not been room for all four pilots as well as Mrs Fellowes in the three aircraft, Clydesdale had returned to Britain from Bombay by sea. He had astonished some of his friends by reappearing without warning at some of his old haunts in London. He received a message from the Provost of Renfrew that on 20th May, as soon as he flew back to Renfrew aerodrome, presentations would be made to him. Clydesdale sent a telegram to him that he much appreciated the kind arrangements for the welcome, and he strongly urged that McIntyre received equal honours.

On their return to Scotland on 20th May, Clydesdale and McIntyre flew in an Air Pageant over Renfrew aerodrome with the other pilots of 602 (City of Glasgow) Squadron. By special arrangement they detached themselves from the formation and landed at an enclosure. There they each received a memorial in the form of an engraving of Everest with their aircraft upon it from Sir Harold Yarrow, President of the Scottish Flying Club. That evening in Renfrew Town Hall, the two men were welcomed by Provost Michie. The applause was loud in recognition of the completion of a mighty task. They had shown that British aircraft and engines could do it, that aerial survey could be carried out in such mountainous territory, and that much had been learned about the apparatus required for high altitude flying. Wrist watches were presented to both of them as a memento on behalf of the East Renfrew Conservative Association.

In response Clydesdale said that the flight had been very much like performing ordinary Royal Air Force duties. The Indians whom they had met had been extremely helpful and had given great assistance. There had been much interest and some superstition amongst those Indians who had never seen an aircraft before. He had been commissioned to drop a message over the Mission School of Dr. Graham, who had been a Moderator of the Church of Scotland. One elderly Indian told Dr. Graham that he was able to depart in peace since he had lived long enough and had at last seen God. On another occasion, an Indian on seeing the aircraft cried out, "The devil in person has arrived". He had learnt a lot about India and was very grateful to have been permitted to take part in the Expedition by the unanimous agreement of his Association. McIntyre also spoke, adding that if qualities of daring, determination and personality had anything to do with politics, then he could congratulate the Association most heartily on their choice of a Member of Parliament.[9]

It was a very warm welcome. On the Saturday evening the 602 City of Glasgow Squadron held a dinner in honour of the Expedition, attended by Lord Provost Swan who expressed the view that nothing greater had been done in their generation. Flight Lieutenant Farquhar, the acting Commanding Officer in Clydesdale's absence, pointed out that if they wanted to fly over any mountains, there was not one in the whole country high enough to stop them.[10]

A few days later on 1st June *The Times* gave a lunch in honour of the Houston Mount Everest Flight Expedition, with the owner of *The Times*, Major Astor, presiding; the guest of honour was the Duke of York, the future King George VI. King George V had a sent a message to *The Times* expressing gladness that his son was able to join in the celebration of the achievements of those "who have so greatly distinguished themselves in the world of adventure". Also attending were the founder of the Royal Air Force, Lord Trenchard, Air Marshal Dowding, who would become Chief of Fighter Command in the Battle of Britain, and Wing Commander Orlebar, who had trained the British pilots who won the Schneider Trophy.

McIntyre and Clydesdale, flanked by General Sir Maxwell Scott and Lord Provost Swan of Glasgow, with Flight-Lieutenant Farquhar in the centre, are welcomed home by 602 (City of Glasgow) Squadron

On behalf of *The Times* the Duke of York presented commemorative silver medals, representing an aeroplane with Everest in the background and with "April 1933" inscribed below, to Clydesdale, Fellowes, Blacker and Ellison. Major Astor, in proposing the toast, said that "No eloquence could do justice to that achievement, to the defiance of nature in her harshest and most relentless form, and to the overcoming of difficulties of organisation and construction".[11] The Secretary of State for India, Sir Samuel Hoare, made a speech in support. Since publication of his White Paper on India, it was the only occasion that he had been able to make a speech in relation to that country on which there was unanimous agreement. They were there to honour a success, well conceived and carried out with efficiency, owing to excellent preparations. This would pave the way for air travel at much higher altitudes.

Air Commodore Fellowes replied that they had gone on their Expedition in a spirit of adventure, and in the days of competition it was useful to the nation to demonstrate the value of its enterprise to the world. They had been very glad to give *The Times* the material which proved that British aircraft and engines were efficient. He paid a tribute to Lady Houston, to the Secretaries of State for Air and India for their assistance and to *The Times* for reporting the developments so fully. He was followed by Squadron Leader Lord Clydesdale, who said that they had a definite job to do and they did it. He too associated himself with the remarks about Lady Houston.[12]

Yet another celebration followed on 14th June when a dinner was given to the members of the Expedition by the Parliamentary Air Committee in the House of Commons Dining Room. With the permission of the Speaker photographs of Everest were displayed on the walls of the dining room. More than 50 M.P.s attended, including Winston Churchill, who was so strongly opposed to the proposals in Sir Samuel Hoare's White Paper on India.

The Prime Minister, Ramsay Macdonald, sent a message saying "I should like to express the admiration which every member of the House of Commons has for Lord Clydesdale and those who were with him in his spirited adventure which has stirred the sporting instincts of the world".[13] He congratulated them on their safe return. The Chairman, Rear Admiral Sueter, added that the flights had shown what British pluck, British pilots and British machines could do. In reply Air Commodore Fellowes in the course of his remarks mentioned that there was an expanding aviation market in India, and Clydesdale spoke of the rude awakening for an M.P. after a three month absence in dealing with 18,000 items of correspondence, much of it from constituents who were members of cooperative societies. Winding up the evening Sir Philip Sassoon, Under Secretary of State for Air, on behalf of the Air Ministry, offered congratulations, stressing that the secret of success had lain in the care and thoroughness of their preparations. But this was not the end of their welcome home.[14]

It was inevitable that at the fourteenth Royal Air Force Display at Hendon Aerodrome on 24th June, the two Westland aircraft which had been over Mount Everest would be exhibited and flown, along with the biplane flown by Cyril Uwins, which had won the world altitude record, and the monoplane piloted by Squadron Leader Gayford which had won the world long distance record. It was hoped that the display involving some two hundred aircraft would emphasise the lead which was held by the British aeronautical engineering industry in world aviation.

These events culminating in the lunch given by *The Times,* the Dinner given in the House of Commons and the Royal Air Force Display, represented the climax of the homecoming. There were of course other events. The main participants were invited to give lectures and the photographs were displayed in public, but the main purposes had been achieved.

A contemporary cartoon: Clydesdale, Burleigh, Churchill and their interests

Far from there being any reservations about Clydesdale for being absent from his constituency for three months, in the ensuing General Election his constituents returned him to the House of Commons with the fifth biggest majority out of Scotland's 71 seats. As was reported in *The Observer* on 4th June 1933: "There are signs that a world too full-fed of words begins to crave for the men of deeds whose example touches a deeper chord. And the proofs are all around us that courage, energy and aspiration are as ready and abundant as ever to enrich the meaning of life."[15]

Ironically, when those words appeared in print, it was on the verge of the only major row which occurred during the whole saga of the Mount Everest Air Expedition. At the centre of it was the lady who had made it all possible. Lady Lucy Houston felt that she had been dreadfully slighted by Major Astor, owner of *The Times*.

12 *LADY LUCY HOUSTON*

LUCY HOUSTON WAS in many respects a character larger than life and in 1933 many regarded her as a modern Boadicea. She kept her age a closely guarded secret, but she was 75 at that time, and much older than she looked. Her impact on the history of British aviation had been substantial and to understand how this happened it is necessary to have an idea of her character.

Born the daughter of a Camberwell boxmaker, she had married the owner of a line of steamers, Sir Robert Houston, who had made a prodigious fortune in the Boer War, shipping hay and oats to South Africa for the British cavalry. He had been devoted to her, and recorded in his will that she had twice nursed him back to life, after the doctor considered that there was nothing they could do for him. In turn she had exerted a great influence over him.

It was rumoured that Sir Robert Houston was intending to leave one million pounds to a distinguished politician. However Lady Houston learned that he had tried to prevent Sir Robert marrying her, and she made sure that he deleted the name of that person from his will. After Sir Robert's death in 1926, the *Oxford Mail* commented in surprise that he had left nothing to "his bosom friend"[1] Lord Birkenhead, and almost everything, some £7 million, to his wife. She had become rich, beyond the dreams of avarice, the second wealthiest woman in Britain, and certainly one of the wealthiest women in the world.

There was some difficulty to be faced in relation to the amount of tax she would have to pay. She went to see the Chancellor of the Exchequer, Winston Churchill, who appeared with the Lord Chancellor, Lord Hailsham. She called him a coward for not having the courage to see her alone. When she came back to see him on the next occasion he did see her alone and she handed over to him a cheque for £1,500,000 payable to the Treasury, later saying that he helped her with the noughts.

Her Secretary wrote of her that

> Like most people she was a bundle of contradictions, but so much was she a woman of extremes that these contradictions were exaggerated to the verge of impossibility. As shy and demure as a schoolgirl when she faced a sympathetic audience, she could be as brazen-faced and coarse-mouthed as a fish-wife in controversy.
>
> A first-rate businesswoman, she was unique among the very rich, having no desire to increase her wealth and making the most of it by spending like royalty on causes that tickled her fancy and seemed to her worth more than money.
>
> She was a terror to work for, often a domineering tyrant, deaf to reason and commonsense, yet possessed of a mysterious charm, which must have been the soul of her youthful beauty, and a capacity for the unexpected, which commanded one's interest and reconciled one to her tantrums and caprices.
>
> For her public enemies, she had neither pity nor mercy . . . Her whole existence was one long protest against Safety First . . . and much of the bitterness and extravagance of her politics arose from her hatred of indecision and cowardice.[2]

She was roused in 1930 by the refusal of the Government to provide the funding for Britain to enter for the Schneider Trophy. This was the seaplane race, which Britain had won in 1927 and in 1929, and required only one further victory to keep the Trophy for good. In January 1931 Lady Houston made herself responsible for the expenses involved in Britain entering for the Schneider Trophy, attacking those in authority for their lack of support, and claiming "This is the sort of insult only a Socialist Government could be guilty of . . ."[3] Britain went on to win the Schneider Trophy, with her help, and later on in the 1930s this victory would have the most far-reaching consequences.

In 1932 she had goaded the Government that London had inadequate air defence. She gained a certain amount of notoriety when she offered £200,000 to the Treasury to provide for forty aircraft. The Prime Minister felt that it would be a reflection on the Government to accept this offer as it might be interpreted as an admission of inadequacy as far as London's defence was concerned. So she published an open letter to the citizens of

London under the heading "Which is most important, the Safety of London or the Imaginary Dignity of the Prime Minister?"[4] She emphasised that London was the only capital without air defence and that the homes of Londoners and their children could be bombed within a few hours. She again offered the £200,000 and urged the people of London to tell the Government to accept the offer. It was to no avail. Neville Chamberlain, as Chancellor of the Exchequer, replied that it was "impossible to earmark any gift to the Treasury".[5]

If Winston Churchill had been Chancellor she would have received a very different reply, and within eight years her warning that London homes could be bombed within hours would come true. Then the country would resent the previous inactivity of their Governments, as much as Lady Houston resented the Government in 1932 for what she believed to be its lack of patriotism.

It was against this background that she had decided to provide the funds for the Everest Expedition. She wanted to strengthen Britain's air defences and therefore felt it to be a patriotic duty to help when approached by the youngest Squadron Leader in the Auxiliary Air Force. His modest manner charmed her. Her hesitation and concern had been due to her fear that the pilots and observers might be killed in the process.

She had been cross to learn that contrary to her instructions and wishes solicitor, Willie Graham, taking with him the Field Service Regulations of the Army. He showed the paragraphs, inspired by the Duke of Wellington, laying down that a formal order must not be departed from when the giver is present. But if the giver was absent, and there was a change of circumstances, the recipient is not only allowed to depart from the letter of the order, but is advised to do so. Willie Graham saw the point and promised to speak to Lady Houston. Her forgiveness was complete, and she sent to Blacker and the other members of the Expedition large boxes of cigars.[6]

It was quite another matter when she learned that Major Astor had refused to read out her statement to *The Times* Lunch which she considered that he had promised to do. She was first and foremost a patriot wishing to conserve a strong and united British Empire, by having an Army, Navy and Air Force strong enough to protect it, its food supplies and trade. She was distrusting of the Government White Paper on India, suspecting that the Government, with the support of *The Times,* might at a later date try to scuttle out of India. When news reached her that her message had not been read out, because it had been censored by Lord Astor, her reaction was immediate.

She had already bought the *Saturday Review* and published her entire correspondence with Major Astor under the headline: "This correspondence reveals to what depths advocates of the White Paper will descend. The searchlight of publicity exposes Major Astor and the Editor of *The Times* AS MEN WHO DARED NOT SPEAK OR PRINT THE TRUTH contained in my message—why I financed the Houston Mount

Everest Expedition."[7] The correspondence published was so vituperative that it is worth quoting at length.

June 12th, 1933.

Dear Major Astor,

On grounds of courtesy—if no more—I think everyone will agree—that when you deliberately suppress a message issued by me—a message you yourself asked me for—some explanation is due to me.

In May 4th last, you wrote and invited me to a complimentary luncheon you were giving to the members of the Houston Mount Everest Expedition on June 1st, but I wired back as follows:—

So sorry my health prevents me accepting your invitation to Luncheon on June 1st, but I shall be pleased to send you a message for you to read out."

Unfortunately my state of health curtails my activities and I was not well enough to immediately write the message I had promised you. However, on May 25th, you wrote me the following letter:—

Dear Lady Houston,

I write to tell you that "The Times" is striking medals in commemoration of the Houston Mount Everest Expedition, one of which will be presented after our Luncheon on June 1st to each of its members. They are the work of Mr. Percy Metcalf. These medals will be given only to the actual participants but I should greatly like you to accept one and if you will permit me, I shall have one struck for you.

YOU WERE GOOD ENOUGH TO SAY THAT YOU WOULD LIKE TO SEND A MESSAGE FOR ME TO READ AT THE LUNCHEON. Yours sincerely,

J. J. Astor.

To this I answered:—

Thank you so much. Delighted to accept medal. Will send message later on.

Lucy Houston.

Thus a clear undertaking was given on my part—although not really well enough to do so—to send you a message for you to read out—and a clear undertaking was given on your part to read out this message at the Luncheon.

But I was only well enough to write it early on the same morning as the Luncheon—and I sent it to you by car at eleven o'clock. The Luncheon was not until 1.30—so that if you had not wished to read it out—you had plenty of time to tell me so—as my chauffeur was instructed to wait for an answer—but when my secretary rang you up to tell you the message was en route—you said you were very glad and would be delighted to read it at the Luncheon.

This was my message:—

WHY I FINANCED THE HOUSTON MOUNT EVEREST EXPEDITION.

When I promised Lord Clydesdale that I would finance this Great Adventure —and he went forth like Jack the Giant Killer—to conquer Everest—many people said "Why does she do it?"

My reason was this—a relation of mine had just come from India and three days after she left—her nearest neighbour was murdered. This sort of thing I was told is—alas—not unusual now in India. I asked "Why?"—and the answer I got was—that since agitators had been permitted to preach treason it has made the people of India think that we Britons have lost our courage—and that they had better therefore stand in with these others.

This made me feel that some great deed of heroism might rouse India and make them remember that though they are of a different Race—they are British Subjects—under the King of England—who is Emperor of India—*and what more can they want?*

For all Indians love brave deeds and must rejoice with us and feel proud of this act of heroism our valiant airmen have accomplished in mounting seven miles into the air over India's highest mountain—for this is surely a proof to them that pluck and courage are not dead in our Race and perhaps—who can tell—this may make them remember all the advantages and privileges they have enjoyed under English Rule—and all the loving kindness that was shown them by our forefathers—who fed them when there was famine—who nursed them when there was plague—and who administered absolute justice to them in every dispute—for as long as our Race exists indomitable courage and an unalterable love of justice will always be our outstanding characteristics, for that great thinker Maeterlinck tells us—"that the character of a Nation never alters."

LUCY HOUSTON.

I was, therefore, furious when late in the afternoon—I was told that my message had not been read out at all by you—but you had only slighly referred to it—and later in the evening you sent me this letter:—

DEAR LADY HOUSTON,

It gives me the greatest pleasure to send you The Times commemorative medal of the Houston Mount Everest Flight Expedition. I feel sure that you will be pleased to hear that my references to your generosity and your message, as well as the tributes paid you by Air Commodore Fellowes and Lord Clydesdale were very warmly received.

Yours sincerely,

JOHN J. ASTOR.

This letter was an insult, and my secretary at once rang up and gave the message I had sent you—to three prominent London newspapers—the *Morning Post*—the *Daily Mail*—and—the *Daily Sketch*—which under the heading—"Why I financed the Houston Mount Everest Expedition" was printed by them the next morning.

But the paper in which it did not appear—was *The Times* newspaper.

Will you kindly tell me what there was in this message that you considered unsuitable for your guests to hear?

It was surely irrelevant to inform me that your references to my generosity in financing the Expedition—as well as those of Air Commodore Fellowes and Lord Clydesdale were warmly received. Pray did you expect the audience to hiss when you mentioned my name?

Did you think it unseemly to remind them that murdering British Officers is now not unsual in India—because agitators are permitted to preach treason—or did you suppose your guests would object to me saying that "as long as the

English Race exists—indomitable courage and an unalterable love of justice will always be our outstanding characteristics"?

I am sometimes very simple for I foolishly imagined that you—the Proprietor of *The Times* newspaper—would be a gentleman—and a man of honour—but had I known you better—I could have given my message to one of my friends to read out—several of whom were at the Luncheon—for naturally everybody at the Luncheon would have liked to hear why I financed this Great Adventure—instead of being told by you an entirely different reason from the one I gave.

The sole publicity rights of the Expedition was given to *The Times* newspaper—I regret to say without my knowledge or consent (because I was too ill at the time my permission was asked to reply). These rights were so valuable that they trebled and quadrupled the circulation of *The Times* and made it a paper everyone wished to buy, and they were the means of giving *The Times* a badly needed fillip in interest—in prestige—as well as in circulation. Before it acquired these rights it was mostly bought only by businessmen who purchased it for its commercial information—for its political policy is still deplorable and only read by defeatists—and yet for these distinct advantages—neither *The Times* newspaper nor its Proprietor has had the grace to thank me.

These unpleasant facts make it all the more astonishing that you should have gone out of your way to insult the woman who paid for all the added prestige your newspaper has reaped from the Houston Mount Everest Expedition.

What have you got to say to this, Major Astor?

LUCY HOUSTON.

On the 16th of June Major Astor sent me this answer:—

DEAR LADY HOUSTON,

I have been away for a few days, or would have replied sooner to your letter of June 12th.

The Luncheon in question was given by the Board of The Times to, and in honour of, the members of the Flight.

It seemed natural to invite you to it, and, as you were unable to come, I should have been glad to convey a message of welcome or congratulation from you to the members of the Expedition.—In the circumstances of the Luncheon I certainly would not have consented to the reading out of a long statement of anyone's views on the British position in India—or indeed on any political matter.

You refer to the publicity rights of the Expedition. This was a business matter between The Times and the Expedition. I do not propose to discuss it here, or any effect which the Flight may have had on The Times or its circulation. I will only say that on this point you must have been misinformed, and the estimate you were apparently given is fantastic.

Everyone must regret that so heroic a feat as the flight over Everest should be followed by the kind of recrimination which your letter suggests. I have no intention of allowing myself to take part in it, and prefer not to take notice of the personal remarks contained in your letter.

Yours truly,
JOHN J. ASTOR.

To which I replied as follows:—

DEAR MAJOR ASTOR,

I have received your letter of the 16th. I cannot congratulate you on your very un-successful attempt to slur over your breach of faith—by ignoring it. . . .

I do not believe any other newspaper Proprietor in London—would have acted so dishonourably. . . .

But what does amuse me is when you say 'In the circumstances of the Luncheon I certainly would not have consented to the reading out of a long statement of anyone's views on the British position in India—or indeed on any political matter.'

Supposing I had been well enough to go to your Luncheon and had stood up and spoken my message. What would you have done? Would you have turned me out? What fun? I am sorry I wasn't there! I wouldn't have missed that for anything! Imagine the Headlines in the Evening Papers—

LADY HOUSTON—WHO FINANCED THE HOUSTON MOUNT EVEREST EXPEDITION—TURNED OUT OF THE LUNCHEON GIVEN TO THE EXPEDITION—BY ORDER OF MAJOR ASTOR—PROPRIE-TOR OF THE TIMES NEWSPAPER—BECAUSE SHE WISHED TO SAY WHY SHE FINANCED THE EXPEDITION!!!

LUCY HOUSTON[8]

She went on to elaborate further grievances. What Lady Houston had overlooked, during the of waging of this vendetta, was that in India the Houston Mount Everest Expedition had received support from Indians all the way across India. The most important assistance in relation to meteorological conditions, in the absence of which the Expedition would have failed, was given by Gupta who was an Indian, so the Indians shared in the success.

In fact the attitude of the Indian people to the first flight over Mount Everest was not dissimilar to that of the rest of the world. Only a few months before, on 15th October 1932, the Indian industrialist J.R.D. Tata flew the first airmail flight in a Puss Moth, flying from Karachi to Bombay. In later years he would found the Tata Airlines and Air India, and on the fiftieth anniversary of his first airmail flight, he flew a Leopard Moth for the golden jubilee flight. On the same day he received a telegram from Mrs. Indira Gandhi as Prime Minister of India, "I salute the spirit of adventure. May you ever remain young at heart. The growth of civil aviation owes much to your pioneering contribution.'[9] The words of the telegram strongly echoed the sentiments expressed after the Everest flight, in India and elsewhere.

As well as Indian support for the Everest Expedition, the Maharajah of Nepal had given invaluable assistance. Without his permission the flight could not have been attempted, and his blessing was all the more welcome as quite a number of Nepalese looked upon Everest as the Home of the Gods. When an earthquake took place in Nepal some months later, it was rumoured that the aeroplanes had stirred up the wrath of the Gods.

Lady Houston also did not understand that the flight would not have the political consequences in India she would have wished. There Mahatma Gandhi was appealing to the national and democratic aspirations of his countrymen, and was stirring the hearts and minds of countless Indians. Winston Churchill referred to him as a 'a half-naked fakir', but for all that Churchill towered over his contemporaries in his will to confront the world's dictators, in Mahatma Gandhi he, and Lady Houston for that matter, had met their match. Gandhi, acting as the father of the Indian nation, was giving impetus to an Independence movement which would one day become irresistible in practice.

Clydesdale was very grateful to Lady Houston for funding the Expedition and in the House of Commons was on the fringe of Churchill's personal circle, sometimes having dinner with him, but he did not accede to Lady Houston's wish and join Churchill in the latter's opposition to the India Bill. This measure gave increased autonomy to the Indian states, and Clydesdale regarded it as a modest constitutional development.

Although the flight had no political impact on India, it had been noticed in other ways. Lady Houston was glad to learn that the American Ambassador to London had said at the City Livery Club that the whole world had been thrilled by the achievements of conquering the unconquerable, and nowhere to a higher degree than in his own country. Wherever men lived who were moved by the spirit of sportsmanship they had been uplifted by the gallant adventurers.[10]

She was even more pleased to hear about Colonel Etherton's audience with the Pope in the Vatican. The Pope had said that the flight had shown that the world's highest mountains were no bar to civil and commercial aviation and that the spirit of adventure was not dead. He gave his blessing to the other members of the Expedition, and particularly to Lady Houston who had made the flight possible. Lady Houston had this information published in the Saturday Review, saying she had been blessed by the Pope for her patriotism and she still awaited a message from the Archbishop of Canterbury.[11]

She felt a measure of recognition when, at the initiative of the Government of Nepal the hot lake discovered on the Southern slopes of Everest was named Parvati Tal, the Lady of the Mountains, to commemorate her patronage.[12] She enjoyed making the speech at the lunch inaugurating the "Wings Over Everest" film, which the Ceylon Observer described as "the most exciting thing of its kind since the Scott Antarctic pictures".[13]

She would have been less pleased to know that the European dictatorships were interested, and among those who were impressed were the leaders of the Nazi Party, who had just come to power in Germany, including Rudolf Hess, Hitler's Deputy, and a man with a fascination for aviation. Although he never met Lady Houston or Clydesdale before the war, the Everest flight was firmly implanted in Hess's memory, a fact which would lead to repercussions eight years later.[14]

In Italy as well there had been interest. General Balbo, the Minister for

Air, had sent a message to Lord Londonderry congratulating him on the successful flight over Mount Everest.[15] Within days, on 10th April, Warrant Officer Agello of the Italian Regia Aeronautica flew a Macchi at 423 mph, establishing a new world speed record, more than 16 mph faster than the previous world record of Flight Lieutenant Stainforth. Italy was challenging Britain's lead in aviation, and it had been precisely for the purpose of meeting such a challenge that Lady Houston had funded Britain's entry for the Schneider Trophy by paying over a cheque for £100,000 to the Royal Aero Club. Funding the Everest Expedition had been her most important contribution since Britain won the cup in 1931 with a high-powered seaplane, the Supermarine S6B flying at 340 mph. This led to the development of the Supermarine Type 224, described as a direct ancestor of the prototype K5054, none other than the Supermarine Spitfire, which turned the balance in the Battle of Britain. When Clydesdale requested permission from his Association to be allowed to participate in the Everest Expedition he had written that the people of Britain did not yet realise what they owed to Lady Houston. This was a reference to the Spitfire being developed, and Lady Houston would have hoped for no better epitaph than that she too had played her part in winning the Battle of Britain.

She died a few days after the Abdication of King Edward VIII. She felt as though a friend had been betrayed and in her fury she would not eat or sleep, becoming ill. At the age of 79 it was too much for her. Her article expressing devotion to the King, using the phrase "Dropping the pilot"[16] was her last as Editor of the *Saturday Review*.

It was fitting that a tribute was paid to her by Air Commodore Fellowes:

As the Leader of the Houston Mount Everest Flight, an Expedition which would never have been launched but for the vivid patriotic imaginings of the late Dame Lucy Houston, may I be allowed to pay my tribute to a most remarkable woman?

She was to me the embodiment of intense patriotism, as she saw it, courage and shrewdness. Her heart was great in its affections and loyalties, and also in its hates. She cannot but leave a blank to friend or enemy so vivid was her personality.[17]

Her support for the Everest Expedition, like that for the Schneider Trophy before it, led on to something else. It laid the foundations for the fulfilment of a dream.

13 *THE FULFILMENT OF A DREAM*

AFTER *THE TIMES* lunch for the members of the Expedition, they parted, going their separate ways. Never again did they meet as a complete gathering. Air Commodore Fellowes retained his interest in flying and Colonel Etherton continued exploring. He even crossed the Atlantic in an airship to Argentina in another record-breaking flight.

As for Colonel Blacker, he had accomplished the task on which he had set his heart for years, and he now settled down to inventing. He devised the Blacker Bombard and what was to become known as the Piat Gun. With these weapons, the projectile was put into the tray of the gun which was used as the bomb projector and was known as the Spigot Mortar Blacker believed it was essential for the British Infantry to have this weapon, to have the capacity to halt any possible *blitzkrieg* by any German Panzer Division. Unhappily the Ministry of Defence reacted too little and too late, and the British Infantry were not equipped with the weapon before Dunkirk. Eventually the Piat gun, for which Blacker was largely responsible, was brought into service in the armies of Britain and the Commonwealth later on in the Second World War. It was of particular value at the Battle of Arnhem, where the Parachute Regiment faced overwhelming odds, and a massed tank attack from the 2nd SS Panzer Corps. The few Piat guns available may well have saved the lives of literally hundreds of soldiers. Although Blacker received little official recognition, he would have been delighted that his invention had proved invaluable, saving the lives of many parachutists.[1]

Blacker occasionally corresponded with Clydesdale and McIntyre, but saw little of them. On their return, the two pilots, after receiving the Air Force Cross, were involved in the fulfilment of their dream. Before leaving for their Expedition Clydesdale had stated that he wished to further the interests of aviation in Britain, and looked forward to the creation of a Scottish Aviation Industry. At that time it appeared in the press as a throwaway line, but he had in fact meant it. Now that they had both flown over Mount Everest they had greater standing as aviators and a better chance of achieving their aim.

Their first step was to find a base and they alighted on the idea of forming a flying school. They knew that the Government was expanding the Royal Air Force without increasing expenditure and were allowing certain groups to open flying schools. Applicants could fly as civilians for the first fifty hours, joining the Royal Air Force to complete their training.

On 9th. August, 1935, Clydesdale and McIntyre, along with Clydesdale's brother Lord George Douglas-Hamilton and the Directors of the De Havilland aircraft company, formed the Scottish College of Aviation Limited. On 12th. February 1936 the name of the company was changed to Scottish Aviation Limited, as its purposes included introducing the aviation industry in its various forms to Scotland as well as tuition in how to fly. Another member of the Everest team, Dick Ellison, associated himself with Clydesdale and McIntyre in this venture, and he and Noel Capper became the first two flying instructors for the company.

A total of 39,000 £1 shares were issued for the company. Clydesdale had persuaded the Hamilton Trustees to invest £17,200, the De Havilland Aircraft Company invested £12,400 and David McIntyre put down £4,200. Clydesdale became its first Chairman, McIntyre the Managing Director and Ellison the Chief Test Pilot.[2]

Prestwick was chosen as the company's location largely because it enjoyed freak fog-free weather conditions. The company acquired land there, near the Orangefield Hotel. At first the aerodrome consisted of 157 acres of land, and then a further 191 acres were bought to accommodate a hangar, offices and a control tower. The Air Ministry approved its use as a flying school operating Tiger Moths, and early in 1936 the first batch of thirty-four pilots were trained. This was only the beginning, for McIntyre had been heard to remark that within ten years Prestwick would have an international airport and an aviation industry.

Gradually activities at Prestwick expanded. In 1937 pilots in the Royal Air Force Volunteer Reserve began to train at Prestwick, being taught to fly Hawker Harts by No. 12 Elementary Flying School. A year later a school for the training of navigators flying in Ansons was opened there, with Scottish Aviation Ltd. servicing aircraft with small parts and doing small-scale modifications to aircraft.

When war broke out in 1939, McIntyre was the Station Commander at Prestwick which immediately became an R.A.F. Station. He closed the road across the aerodrome, doubling its size overnight. By the end of 1940 Prestwick had been selected as the best aerodrome in Britain for aircraft crossing the Atlantic. Previously aircraft were transferred from the U.S.A. to Canada, where they took off from Newfoundland and then landed at Aldergrove in Northern Ireland. Transatlantic crossing by Liberators steadily increased, and McIntyre recommended that the runway be increased to 2,200 yards in length. After a struggle with the Air Ministry, he got his way, receiving Canadian support. The Orangefield Hotel was taken over by the Air Ministry, and it had a Control Tower built into its roof, the Hotel becoming the Terminal Mess.

A reunion of some of the participants in 1944: Blacker, McIntyre, Bonnett and Ellison

The Scottish Aviation factory which had appeared so modestly before the war, began to expand by leaps and bounds. Soon there would be more than one thousand transatlantic crossings in and out of Prestwick each month. The Palace of Engineering at Bellahouston Park, Glasgow, had been moved to Prestwick. This had been a terrific effort, and many had thought it would not be possible. Within the new building Scottish Aviation Ltd. might be able to repair and adapt the numerous aircraft coming into Prestwick, including Spitfires, Hurricanes, Liberators,

Prestwick Pioneers and Twin Pioneers in flight

Hudsons, Skuas, Rocs and Lysanders, to mention but a few of the many aircraft involved. Employing hundreds of persons, including Ellison as Chief Test Pilot and latterly as General Manager, as well as Francis Burnard, the Westland representative during the Everest Expedition, Scottish Aviation was performing a function essential to the war effort.[3]

In the latter half of the war McIntyre and Clydesdale were Group Captains, Clydesdale having succeeded his father as Duke of Hamilton in 1940. While McIntyre remained Station Commander at Prestwick, after acting as a controller in the HQ of 11 Group Fighter Command, Hamilton became Station Commander at Turnhouse and was responsible for the air defence of much of the Central Belt of Scotland. Thereafter he became Commandant of the Air Training Corps in Scotland. Towards the end of the war, though, Hamilton learnt that McIntyre, after an astonishing series of successes, had run into opposition. They had hoped that Prestiwick would be designated as an international airport, but the British Government, under the influence of Sir Stafford Cripps, decided that only Heathrow should be given such a status. This, of course, would cause much international traffic to be diverted away from Prestwick to Shannon in Eire, where Charles Lindbergh would act as adviser.

Together McIntyre and Hamilton welcomed Tom Johnston, who had a reputation as a strong Secretary of State for Scotland, to Prestwick. They put Prestwick's case to him pointing out that services were available there for twenty-four hours of the day. Tom Johnston's assistance may well have led to the designation of Prestwick in 1946, as Britain's second international airport.

Earlier, in 1945, McIntyre was asked to produce a design for a small military reconnaissance aircraft. It was a request which would have important implications for Scottish Aviation. The end of the war had brought with it a period of uncertainty. McIntyre had hoped to operate a civil airline, and for some time succeeded in doing so, but nationalisation compelled him to concentrate on aircraft manufacture. He produced, with his growing workforce, the Prestwick Pioneer and Twin Pioneer, which had a short take-off and landing capacity. It was a brilliant invention and the Ministry of Defence ordered many for use in Malaya. At the Farnborough Air Show Hamilton sold many of them to Portugal, and Pioneers were sold to other countries, including Ceylon.[4] Later on Scottish Aviation would build the Bulldog training aircraft, and would service many aircraft, including CF104 Starfighters, belonging to the Canadian Air Force among others.

Hamilton and McIntyre always remained great friends. In the 1930s Hamilton had been most in the public eye as a Scottish Member of Parliament, but McIntyre succeeded him as Commanding Officer of the 602 City of Glasgow Squadron and in the late 1940s and 1950s McIntyre's name was associated with Prestwick more than anybody else, Hamilton's support as Chairman of Scottish Aviation being in the background. In fact each man owed a great deal to the other and neither man could have achieved what he did without the other's support.

By the early 1950s the Scottish Aviation Industry had become a major source of employment in Scotland. Within fifty years of their flight over Everest, Scottish Aviation, after a number of mergers, had become the Scottish Division of British Aerospace, employing more than 2,000 persons at Prestwick and responsible for building the Jetstream Executive aircraft. Nearby Caledonian Air Motive employ several hundred persons, repairing jet engines.

When Hamilton and McIntyre flew over Mount Everest, they had come within a hair's breadth of disaster, and come through by courage, discipline and judgement. They had only succeeded because they had prepared for the difficulties they would have to surmount. It would not always be so. Shortly after their flights over Everest a young Englishman called Maurice Wilson set off for India. He planned to excel the aviators and the climbers by landing an aircraft high up near Everest, climbing the remainder of the distance on foot with oxygen. He had won the Military Cross in the First World War, and believed he could do it. If only he had spoken to Hugh Ruttledge, he could have been warned that what he was attempting was well beyond the bounds of possibility. On 9th July 1934 Eric Shipton, leading an Everest climbing expedition, came across his body on the East Rongbuk Glacier, at least 8000 feet from the summit of Everest. He had died from cold and exhaustion.[5]

The founders of Scottish aviation and Prestwick, Group Captain David McIntyre AFC, Group Captain the Duke of Hamilton AFC, and their accountant Mr Carlyle Gifford at Prestwick, which would become Britain's second international airport, 1946

Hamilton and McIntyre had not attempted to emulate the mountaineers but they were only too well aware that advances in aviation often took place at the cost of human life. In 1910, in a Bleriot monoplane, Chavez had taken off from Brig in Switzerland to fly over the Alps to Italy. He was the first man to do so, but his aircraft crashed in the process and he did not survive.

In 1957 Hamilton received the tragic news that McIntyre, flying a Prestwick Pioneer in North Africa, had been killed. The Pioneer had developed metal fatigue, a wing broke off and it plunged to the ground. He had not only lost a great friend, but had and would have flying misfortunes in his own family. Two of his three brothers, all of whom joined the Royal Air Force, lost their lives in air crashes. His brother David, who had commanded a Spitfire Squadron in the height of the Blitz over Malta, had been killed after being shot up by German anti-aircraft fire over France in 1944. And his brother, Malcolm, who had won the Military OBE and the Distinguished Flying Cross disappeared in a huge storm around Mount Cameroon in 1964, with his son Neil, after flying across the Atlantic to Africa. Like Mallory's ice axe found by Hugh Ruttledge's expedition in 1933, the wreckage of the aircraft was not discovered until years later.

In spite of these tragedies aviation remained the theme of Hamilton's life, and in 1966 he was asked to chair a Government Commission into the training of Civil Airline pilots by Prime Minister Harold Wilson. Its recommendations were implemented, and he became the President of the British Airline Pilots Association, whose members were the most highly paid British Trade Unionists.

Towards the end of his life, on 25th January 1973, he went to Prestwick and saw in the new Terminal building the plaque: "In honour and memory of David F. McIntyre A.F.C., Burgess of the Burgh of Prestwick whose courageous foresight and acumen led to the founding of Prestwick Airport". He unveiled another plaque to commemorate the Orangefeld Hotel and Terminal Building, in the form of a map showing with an orange mark on the taxi track the site which had performed such an important role in the Second World War, and had been the home of Prestwick's beginnings.[6]

He and McIntyre might so easily not have survived their flight over Everest, but each of them with the other members of the Expedition had a powerful subconscious motive, that Britain had a role to play in aviation, not only to benefit their own countrymen but also the rest of the world. Britain was their home, and Mount Everest provided them with their opportunity.

An aviation industry in Scotland was the legacy which they left their country. Even if they had not done that and had not lived to see the fulfilment of their dream, they would still be remembered. For Britain has not lost its ardour for adventure, and there will always be admiration for young men of courage who are willing to risk their lives to face the perils of the unknown.

The Pioneer's capacity to take off with a very short runway made it much in demand

APPENDICES

1. *Permission to fly over Mount Everest:* Information that the Maharajah of Nepal had given permission for the flight over Everest was sent by the India Office to Colonel Stewart Blacker OBE on 3rd August, 1932.

C O P Y

INDIA OFFICE,
Whitehall,
London, S.W.1.
3rd August, 1932.

Ref: P.Z.4170/32.

Confidential.

Sir,

      With reference to your letter of the 25th May and in continuation of this Office letter of the 1st June, No. P.Z.3103/32, I am directed by the Secretary of State for India to inform you that the permission of the Government of Nepal has been obtained for the carrying out of a flight over their territory with a view to your making a photographic survey of the Southern slopes of Mount Everest. The flight will be permitted subject to the following conditions:

(1)   The aircraft must fly direct to Everest and back without any deviation or landing on the territory of Nepal.

(2)   Neither the Government of Nepal nor its subjects will be held responsible in any way for any untoward event arising out of the flight or, in the event of a forced landing, for any loss of life or injury to the aviators or the machine at the hands of the local population.

(3)   The British Government must satisfy themselves that the intentions of the organisers of the expedition are such as to comply with the Nepal Government's wishes and that the flight without landing in Nepalese territory is reasonably practicable apart from unforeseen accidents, and must take the responsibility for any mishap that may occur.

(4)   The permission granted in this case, purely for scientific purposes, must not be regarded as a precedent but must be treated as exceptional.

(5)   The Maharaja of Nepal is to be given due intimation of the expected departure of the aeroplane from the aerodrome and of its return.

(6)   Copies of the observations and notes taken during the flight are to be supplied to His Highness.

(7) The machine is to fly as high as possible, and <u>as little as possible over Nepalese territory</u>.

2.   The Secretary of State will be glad to receive from <u>you</u>, in due course, <u>an intimation of your acceptance</u> of these conditions, so far as they concern you.

3.   The Government of India have also agreed to your making use of the landing ground at Purnea.

4.   I am also to refer to your letter of the 1st June in which you apply for exemption from British Indian Customs Duties of the equipment and material which your expedition propose to import into India and to inform you in reply that the Government of India are prepared to exempt the equipment, etc. from Customs Duty provided that information is given to them in advance as to the date and port of arrival and the mode of entry into India (whether by sea air or land) in order that appropriate instructions may be issued to the authorities concerned.

5.   It would be convenient if additional details could be furnished of the shipping arrangements contemplated for the stores and equipment if they are not to accompany the expedition, viz:- a complete list of the articles imported, and the name of the ship, numbers and markings of the cases, and the names of the forwarding agents and consignees.

I am, Sir,
Your obedient Servant,
(Sgd) J.C. Walton.

To L. V. S. Blacker, Esq.

2. *The handwritten Report of the Chief Pilot, Squadron Leader the Marquis of Clydesdale MP* after the first flight over Mount Everest on 3rd April, 1933. The corrections on pages 1 and 2 may have been inserted by the Chief Observer, Colonel Blacker.

The Report of the Flight over Mt Everest is told in the following message from S/L Lord Clydesdale to the Times.

RAJ DARBHANGA.

On the morning of the April 3rd, the Indian Met Officer S.N Gupta, at Purnea, whose information and advice has been of very great value to the Expedition reported from balloon observations that the wind which previously had been unsuitable, had dropped to a velocity of 57 m.p.h at 33,000 feet, which altitude we had decided was one most suitable working height for photographic survey.

Our two machines took-off at 8.25 from Lal Balu Aerodrome in still air. The Houston-Westland crewed by Col Blacker and myself and the Westland-Wallace piloted by F/L DF McIntyre with Mr SR Bonnett and photographer of British Gaumont, as observer.

Our direct route to the point was flying on a track of 342°. This necessitated changing the compass course at intervals more to the West, on account of the increase of wind velocity with height, according to our report. We had relied on overcoming to some extent the difficulty of accurate compass navigation, caused by this frequent

2.

RAJ DARBHANGA.

change of wind speed, by the good land-marks near and along our track. A heavy dust haze rising to a considerable altitude almost completely obscured the ground from Forbes Ganj to the higher mountain ranges. This made ~~aerial~~ *ariel.* survey work ~~so~~

X impossible.

We climbed slowly at low engine revs to a height of 10,000 feet. By this height the crew of both men had tested their respective electrical heating and *sets* ~~the electrical~~ . F/l McIntyre and I signaled to each other that everything was satisfactory.

After 30 mins flying we passed over Forbes Ganj *our forward emergency landing fd 40 miles fm P,* and at a height of ~~20,000~~ *19,000* feet Everest first became visible above the haze.

We flew lower than our intended working height (35,000) in order to make every endeavour to pass ~~near to~~ *over* Komaltar close to which is the ~~two point~~ *ground control* ~~from which~~ we were to begin our survey. It ~~however~~ proved impossible to identify any

3.

RAJ DARBHANGA.

landmarks ~~ground~~ at. all until approx within 20 miles of the summit.
At 9.00 we passed over Chamlang at an altitude of 31,500 feet.
On approaching Lotse, the Southern peak of the Everest group.
the ground rises at a steep gradient and both men
due to the deflection of the west win
experienced a steady down current (~~from the wind off~~ lower
dispite our efforts to climb⊙ the mtn.
giving a loss of altitude of 1500 feet ∧ Both aeroplanes
flew over the summit at 10.05 o'clock, clearing it by 500 feet.

The wind velocity was noticeably high near the summit,
but no bumps were felt by either aircraft. 15 mins was
on account of
spent flying in the neighbourhood of the summit. and ~~owing~~
~~to~~ the smooth flying conditions, the taking of close range
photos was rendered possible.

Visibility of distant high peaks was very good.
The Great Himalaya Range could be seen extending to

4

RAJ DARBHANGA.

great distances and provided a magnificent spectical .

The return journey was carried out at a slightly lower altitude, so as to ~~produce~~ secure better conditions for ~~the~~ oblique photography . Both m/cs landed at Lal Bola at 11.25

~~The Engines and Airplanes functioned splendidly throughout the ~~~~ flight .~~

Both pilots pay the highest tributes to the splendid perfce of both engines & aircraft.

3. *Letter from Air Commodore Fellowes DSO,* leader of the Expedition to the Duchess of
Hamilton, mother of the Chief Pilot. Dated 18th April, 1933, it expresses grave
disappointment that a second Everest flight was forbidden.

THE HOUSTON - MT. EVEREST FLIGHT,

PURNEA,

BIHAR,

INDIA.

18th April, 1933.

Dear Duchess,

Thank you most awfully for your two charming
telegrams.   It was sweet of you to send them.

Please forgive me typing this letter to you,
but I am in bed with a mild type of some Indian fever.

I am so sorry you had those anxious moments
about the oxygen gear, but as long as one's mask fits all
right it is absolutely efficient, and you need have no fears.

We are all a very happy party out here, and
are all fit and extraordinarily well.

You very kindly thanked me for my infinite
care, but I can assure you that Clydesdale himself, with his
wonderful thoroughness and care for detail, has been an inspir-
ation to the whole expedition.   Nothing is too much trouble
for him when it comes to getting down to actual preparations,
and his determination to succeed in whatever he attempts is
outstanding.   There is no doubt about it he has got a great
career in front of him.   He seems to like the Indians very
much, and they appear to reciprocate.   Who knows; perhaps
this may be the forerunner of his holding some great post out
here.   He certainly has that very necessary gift of charm,
which perhaps misleads some people as to the determination of
purpose lying behind it, which is perhaps just as well.

You will probably have learned by now that Lady
Houston has stuck her toes in and forbidden a second flight.
This has disappointed us all terribly, as we had everything
ready for the second flight over Everest and no doubt would have
secured really excellent survey results, always supposing there
had been no clouds.   This is the one thing which the expedition
so far has failed to secure.   We all of course expected Clydesdale
and MacIntyre to pilot their aircraft with complete success over
Everest.   What we were not sure of was Colonel Blacker's capacity
to act as photographer, and in this we were very pleasantly surprised; he obtained as good photographs as I think anybody could
have got.   This is much to his credit, and with his vivid power
of expression he must have collected a very large store of useful
information for the book which has yet to be written.

Not only the flying side, but the Gaumont-British
film personnel and the whole staff have shown themselves to be
extraordinarily well chosen for the purposes of the expedition.
As an instance, Mr. Fisher, who came with me over Kanchenjunga,
had never actually been tested at great heights before.   Of course

he had the results of all the experience the others had gained, but he had never been above 20,000 in his life before; in spite of this he acted as if he made a daily business of going over these high mountains: and not only that, but when we had our unpremeditated forced landing and were surrounded by thousands of inquisitive and unruly Indians, he showed himself to be an absolute master in controlling crowds. I only give him as an instance of what all the others are like.

We are much looking forward to our flight home, and probably when we get there Clydesdale's aeroplane will return to meet him at Marseilles or wherever he disembarks, so that he may cross France by air also.

He has remained supremely fit and full out throughout the whole tour, as have all the others with the exception of one or two of the older ones who had minor complaints.

With my kindest regards to the Duke and yourself,

Yours very sincerely,

Peregrine F. M. Fellowes

Her Grace The Duchess of Hamilton and Brandon,

Ferne House,

Shaftesbury.

4. *Seating Plan for the House of Commons Dinner in honour of the Mount Everest Flight Expedition,* Wednesday, 14th June, 1933. The Marquis of Clydesdale MP is sitting next to Winston Churchill, the future Prime Minister who greatly respected Lady Houston. By special permission the main diningroom was used to welcome them.

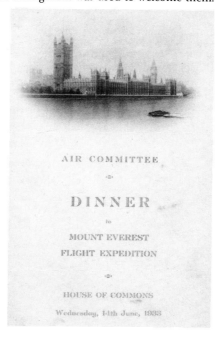

AIR COMMITTEE

DINNER

to

MOUNT EVEREST
FLIGHT EXPEDITION

HOUSE OF COMMONS
Wednesday, 14th June, 1933

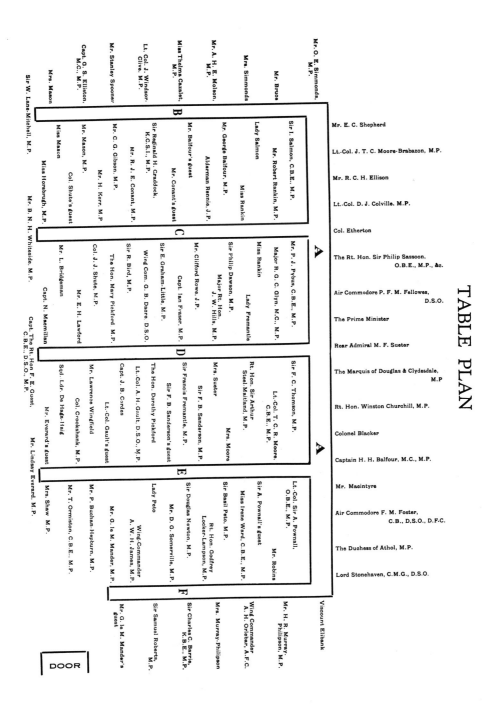

5. *The letter of thanks to Dame Lucy Houston DBE,* dated 31st July, 1934, and signed by the main participants of the Expedition, Colonel Blacker OBE, Air Commodore Fellowes DSO, Colonel Etherton, Flight Lieutenant David McIntyre and Squadron Leader the Marquis of Clydesdale.

TELEPHONE: GROSVENOR 6363.

TELEGRAMS: AEROCOLL, LONDON.

COMMITTEE:
THE RT. HON. THE EARL PEEL, P.C.,G.C.S.I.,G.B.E.
THE RT. HON. THE EARL OF LYTTON, P.C.,G.C.S.I.,G.C.I.E.
THE MARQUIS OF CLYDESDALE, M.P. (CHIEF PILOT)
COLONEL THE MASTER OF SEMPILL, A.F.C.,F.R.AES.
COLONEL JOHN BUCHAN, C.H.,M.P.
WING COMMANDER A.H.ORLEBAR,A.F.C.,ROYAL AIR FORCE.
L.V. STEWART BLACKER,O.B.E.,F.R.G.S.
HON. TREASURER:
THE VISCOUNT BURNHAM, G.C.M.G.,C.H.,LL.D.
EXECUTIVE OFFICER:
AIR COMMODORE P.F.M. FELLOWES, D.S.O.
HON. SECRETARY:
COLONEL P. T. ETHERTON.

THE HOUSTON — MT. EVEREST FLIGHT,

GROSVENOR HOUSE,

PARK LANE, W.1.

ALL COMMUNICATIONS TO BE ADDRESSED TO THE HON. SECRETARY.

College of Aeronautical Engineering,
Sydney Street,
S.W.3.

July 31.1934.
=============

Dear Dame Lucy,

We enclose herewith a cheque for £4949/13/6, which it was understood should be refunded to you from the amount you so generously provided.

In doing this we wish to express to you our sincere appreciation of all you did in financing the Everest Flight, and for your sound advice and assistance which enabled us to go ahead with, and carry out, our plans. We are most grateful to you for the confidence you showed in us, and we shall always look back with feelings of the keenest gratitude and recognition of your action, and the outstanding and memorable rôle you played in the venture.

With our united good wishes that you may long continue to be the great protagonist of British aviation and all that concerns the welfare of the British Empire.

Yours sincerely,

SELECT BIBLIOGRAPHY

1. *Primary Sources.*
The contemporary papers still in existence, relating to the First Flight over Mount Everest are in the posession of the Duke of Hamilton, Brian and David Blacker and Richard Ellison.

In addition a great deal of information about the purposes of the Expedition and its nature was published in Britain, the Commonwealth, the USA and in Europe. This was due in large measure to the fact that Mr Shepherd, the Aviation correspondent of *The Times* flew out to India with the participants and accompanied them throughout.

As well as giving very full coverage in its columns, *The Times* showed the first photographs of Mount Everest's summit taken from above it, and extremely good reproductions which appeared in *The Times* and in the *Illustrated London News,* were published in many countries throughout the world.

2. *Memoirs and Secondary Works,* containing or making use of original material.
ALLEN, WARNER, *Lucy Houston DBE* (Constable and Company Ltd 1947)
BARKER, RALPH, *The Schneider Trophy Races* (Chatto and Windus 1971)
BLACKER, STEWART, *Pathans, Planes and Petards* (unpublished)
BUCHAN, JOHN, *The Last Secrets, The Final Mysteries of Exploration* (Thomas Nelson and Sons Ltd 1941)
BURGE, Squadron Leader, *The Air Annual of the British Empire 1933-34*
CHANT, CHRISTOPHER, *Aviation: An Illustrated History* (Orbis 1978)
CLYDESDALE and McINTYRE, *The Pilot's Book of Everest* (William Hodge and Company Ltd 1936)
COBLE, H and PAYNE, A.R., *Famous Aircraft* (W.R. Chambers 1937)
DORMAN, GEOFFREY, *Fifty Years Fly Past: From Wright Brothers to Comet* (Forbes Robertson 1951)
ENCYCLOPAEDIA BRITTANICA, *Everest*

ETHERTON, Colonel P.T., *The Last Strongholds* (Jarrolds 1934)
FELLOWES, Air Commodore P.F.M., *First Over Everest: The Houston Mount Everest Expedition 1933* (John Lane, the Bodley Head Ltd 1933)
GIBBS-SMITH, CHARLES H., *Aviation: Air Historical Survey from its Origins to the End of World War II* (HMSO 1970)
GILLIES, J.D. and WOOD, J.L., *Aviation in Scotland* (Glasgow Branch of the Royal Aeronautical Society 1966)
HUNT, JOHN, *The Ascent of Everest* (Hodder and Stoughton 1953), *Our Everest Adventure* (Brockhampton Press 1954)
MONDEY, DAVID, *The Schneider Trophy* (Robert Hale 1975)
MURRAY, W.H., *The Story of Everest* (J.M. Dent and Sons 1953)
PENROSE, HARALD, *British Aviation—Widening Horizons 1930-1934* (HMSO)
RUTTLEDGE, HUGH, *Everest 1933* (Hodder and Stoughton Ltd 1934)
SAUNDERS, HILARY St. GEORGE, *Per Ardua, The Rise of British Air Power 1911-1939* (Oxford University Press 1944)
SINHA, The Hon. RAJA KIRTYANAND, *Purnea—A Shikar Land* (Thacker, Spink and Co 1916)
TAPPER, OLIVER, *The World's Great Pioneer Flights* (The Bodley Head 1975)
TAYLOR, JOHN W.R. and MUNSON, KENNETH, *History of Aviation* (New English Library 1972)
TAYLOR, J.W.R., *The Guinness Book of Air Facts and Feats*
TURNER, JOHN FRAYN, *Famous Flights* (Arthur Barker 1978)
VERNE, JULES, *From Earth to Moon and a Trip Round it* (Sampson, Low, Marston & Co Ltd 1936)
WALBANK, F. ALAN, *Wings of War* (Batsford)
WINCHESTER, CLARENCE ed., *Wonders of World Aviation Vol I* (The Waverley Book Co c.1939)

3. *Articles in Periodicals*
The Houston-Everest Expedition, *Flight* 16 February 1933
The Houston-Everest Air Expedition, *Flight* 23 February 1933
The Houston-Everest Expedition, *Flight* 23 March 1933
The Houston-Everest Expedition, *Flight* 30 March 1933
Everest Conquered, *Aeroplane* 5 April 1933
Mount Everest Conquered, *Flight* 6 April 1933
Everest Conquered, *Aeroplane* 12 April 1933
A Second Flight over Everest, *Aeroplane* 26 April 1933
A Second Flight over Everest, *Flight 4 May 1933*
The Everest Lunch, *Aeroplane* 7 June 1933
The Times Honours the Everest Fliers, *Flight* 8 June 1933
LEWIS, BRENDA RALPH, *First Flight over Everest,* Aircraft Illustrated July 1978
WEBB, PETER, *First over Everest,* Aeroplane Monthly April 1982
The Conquest of Everest, *The Bristol Review*
Bristol's First Winged Horse, *The Rolls-Royce Magazine* No. 12

SOURCES

Chapter 1
1. *The Statesman,* Calcutta, 5 and 6 April 1933
2. *Rhodesian Herald,* Salisbury, 14 October 1932
3. *The Statesman,* Calcutta, 5 April 1933
4. John Hunt, *The Ascent of Everest,* p.8
5. Clydesdale & McIntyre, *The Pilot's Book of Everest,* p.7
6. Stewart Blacker, *Pathans, Planes and Petards,* (unpublished) p.79
7. Letter from John Longley, 13th October 1982
8. Fellowes, Blacker, Etherton & Clydesdale: *First Over Everest, The Houston-Mount Everest Expedition 1933,* p.245-9
9. Clydesdale & McIntyre, *The Pilot's Book of Everest* p.9
10. *Paisley and Renfrew Gazette,* 24 September 1932
11. Clydesdale & McIntyre, *The Pilot's Book of Everest* p.10

Chapter 2
1. Clydesdale & McIntyre, *The Pilot's Book of Everest* p.9
2. *The Times,* and *The Scotsman,* 6 October 1932
3. Clydesdale & McIntyre, *The Pilot's Book of Everest* p.13
4. Ibid, p.14
5. *Tangier Gazette* 21 October 1932;
   Evening Telegram, St John's, Newfoundland 25 October 1932
   Civil & Military Gazette, Lahore, India, 9 November 1932
6. Fellowes, Blacker, Etherton & Clydesdale: *First Over Everest, The Houston-Mount Everest Expedition 1933,* p.226,7

Chapter 3
1. *Sunday Express,* 22 January 1933
2. Fellowes, Blacker, Etherton & Clydesdale: *First Over Everest, The Houston-Mount Everest Expedition 1933,* Chapter 3
3. Clydesdale & McIntyre, *The Pilot's Book of Everest* p.15
4. Fellowes, Blacker, Etherton & Clydesdale: *First Over Everest, The Houston-Mount Everest Expedition 1933,* p.16, 75
5. *Biggleswade Chronicle,* 10 March 1933
6. *Mayo News,* Westport, USA 25 March 1933
7. *Nottingham Guardian* 27 March 1933
8. *The Scotsman,* 17 February 1933
9. *Daily Express* 8 March 1933
10. *Glasgow Weekly Herald* 18 March 1933
11. Fellowes, Blacker, Etherton & Clydesdale: *First Over Everest, The Houston-Mount Everest Expedition 1933,* p.112

Chapter 4
1. Clydesdale & McIntyre, *The Pilot's Book of Everest,* p.24, 25
2. Ibid, p. 26, 27
3. Ibid, p. 27, 28
4. Ibid, p.30, 31
5. Ibid, p.36
6. Ibid, p.40, 41

7. Ibid, p.44, 45
8. Ibid, p.45
9. Ibid, p.48

Chapter 5
1. *Book of Reviews,* May 1933
2. Fellowes, Blacker, Etherton & Clydesdale: *First over Everest, The Houston-Mount Everest Expedition 1933,* p.132
3. Ibid, p.160
4. Clydesdale & McIntyre, *The Pilot's Book of Everest,* p.55, 56
5. Ibid, p. 64, 65
6. *North Mail,* Newcastle, *Men Behind Conquest of Everest,* 6 May 1933
7. Clydesdale & McIntyre, *The Pilot's Book of Everest,* p.54, 75, 76
8. Ibid, p.80, 81

Chapter 6
1. *The Times,* 1 April 1933
2. Clydesdale & McIntyre, *The Pilot's Book of Everest,* p.83
3. Ibid, p.94
4. Ibid, p.98, 99
5. Ibid, p.116
6. Ibid, p.100, 101
7. Ibid, p.104
8. Ibid, p.123

Chapter 7
1. Clydesdale & McIntyre, *The Pilot's Book of Everest,* p.126, 7, 141
2. Fellowes, Blacker, Etherton & Clydesdale: *First over Everest, The Houston-Mount Everest Expedition 1933,* p.243
3. Clydesdale & McIntyre, *The Pilot's Book of Everest,* p.129, 130
4. Ibid, p.133, 134
5. Fellowes, Blacker, Etherton & Clydesdale: *First over Everest, The Houston-Mount Everest Expedition 1933,* p.188
6. Clydesdale & McIntyre, *The Pilot's Book of Everest,* p.144
7. Ibid, p.145, 6
8. Fellowes, Blacker, Etherton & Clydesdale: *First over Everest, The Houston-Mount Everest Expedition 1933,* p.189
9. Clydesdale & McIntyre, *The Pilot's Book of Everest,* p.135, 136
10. Fellowes, Blacker, Etherton & Clydesdale: *First over Everest, The Houston-Mount Everest Expedition 1933,* p.189
11. Clydesdale & McIntyre, *The Pilot's Book of Everest,* p.137

Chapter 8
1. *Times Educational Supplement,* 8 April 1933
2. *Newcastle Daily Journal,* 5 April 1933
3. *The Times,* 4 April 1933
4. Ibid
5. *Aeroplane,* London, 12 April 1933
6. *The Scotsman,* 5 April 1933
7. Ibid

8. *Times Weekly Edition,* 6 April 1933
9. *The Scotsman,* 5 April 1933
10. *Aeroplane,* London, 12 April 1933
11. *The Scotsman,* 5 April 1933
12. *Aeroplane,* London, 12 April 1933
13. Ibid
14. *The Scotsman,* 5 April 1933
15. *Daily Record,* 4 April 1933
16. *Yorkshire Observer,* 4 April 1933
17. Confirmed by the Ministry of Defence, Air Historical Branch in a letter dated 26 October 1982
18. *Hindu,* Madras, 4 April 1933
19. *Times of India,* Bombay, 5 April 1933
20. *Ceylon Observer,* 4 April 1933
21. *Central European Times,* Zurich, 10 April 1933
22. *West Middlesex Gazette,* 8 April 1933
23. *Leicester Mail,* 4 April 1933
24. *East Anglian Daily Times,* 5 April 1933
25. *The Times,* 4 April 1933
26. *Montreal Daily Star,* 4 April 1933
27. *Manchester Evening Chronicle,* 4 April 1933
28. *Nottingham Journal,* 4 April 1933
29. *Press,* Christchurch, New Zealand, 5 April 1933
30. *Morning Post,* London, 5 April 1933, (also in the *Saturday Review*)

Chapter 9
1. This account is taken directly from that of Mr Richard Ellison in his letter of 3 September 1982. The accounts given elsewhere as in *First over Everest* were more sensational and not accurate.
2. Fellowes, Blacker, Etherton & Clydesdale: *First Over Everest, The Houston-Mount Everest Expedition 1933,* p.201, 202
3. Ibid, p.202, 203
4. Clydesdale & McIntyre, *The Pilot's Book of Everest,* p.152
5. Ibid, p.104-107
6. Ibid, p.123
7. Ibid, p.156

Chapter 10
1. Clydesdale & McIntyre, *The Pilot's Book of Everest,* p.161
2. Ibid, p.163
3. Ibid, p.163
4. Ibid, p.164
5. Ibid, p.166, 167
6. *The Times* and *Glasgow Herald,* 21 April 1933
7. *Manchester Guardian,* 25 April 1933
8. *The Times,* 24 April 1933
9. *Huddersfield Examiner,* 21 April 1933
   Portsmouth Evening News, 21 April 1933

Chapter 11
  1. *Saturday Review,* 27 June 1936
  2. Clydesdale & McIntyre, *The Pilot's Book of Everest,* p. 174, 190
  3. Letter from Lord Hunt, dated 28 September 1982
  4. Clydesdale & McIntyre, *The Pilot's Book of Everest,* Chapters X and XI
     The Times, 20 April 1933 and 27 May 1933
     Jersey Evening Post, 20 April 1933
     Fellowes, Blacker, Etherton & Clydesdale, *First Over Everest, The Houston-Mount Everest Expedition 1933,* p.227-231
  5. Fellowes, Blacker, Etherton & Clydesdale, *First Over Everest, The Houston-Mount Everest Expedition 1933,* p.216
  6. Etherton, *The Last Strongholds,* p.285
  7. Ibid, p.289
  8. Letter of Mr Richard Ellison, dated 3 September 1982
  9. *The Scotsman,* 22 May 1933
 10. *Daily Record,* 5 June 1933
 11. *Times Weekly Edition,* 8 June 1933
 12. Ibid
 13. *The Times,* 15 June 1933
 14. Ibid
 15. *Observer,* London 4 June 1933

Chapter 12
  1. *Oxford Mail,* 30 December 1936
  2. Lucy Houston DBE, *A Memoir* (Constable) 1947, p.11
  3. Ibid, p.14
  4. Ibid, p.142
  5. *Daily Express,* 30 December 1936
  6. Stewart Blacker, *Pathans, Planes and Petards* (unpublished) p.88
  7. *Saturday Review,* 15 July 1933
  8. Ibid
  9. Telco Parivar, *The Internal House Journal of Telco Pune* Vol 12, No.11, November 1982, p.11
 10. *The Times,* 11 October 1933
 11. *Saturday Review,* 21 April 1934
 12. Ibid, 27 June 1936
 13. *Ceylon Observer,* 1 July 1934
 14. Douglas-Hamilton, James: *Motive for a Mission, The Story Behind Hess's Flight to Britain* (Mainstream Publishing and Corgi)
 15. *The Times,* early April 1933
 16. Allen, Warner, *Lucy Houston DBE, One of the Few,* p.169, 170
 17. Ibid, p.173

Chapter 13
  1. Stewart Blacker, *Pathans, Planes and Petards* (unpublished) p.103
  2. Alan C. Robertson: *History of Scottish Aviation Ltd* (unpublished), Part I, p.3
  3. Wing Commander N.J. Capper AFC, *Prestwick 1935-75,* p.17
  4. Papers of Duke of Hamilton
  5. *News Chronicle,* London 4 June 1936
  6. Wing Commander N.J. Capper AFC, *Prestwick 1935-75,* p.19

INDEX

(Italicized numbers denote photographs)